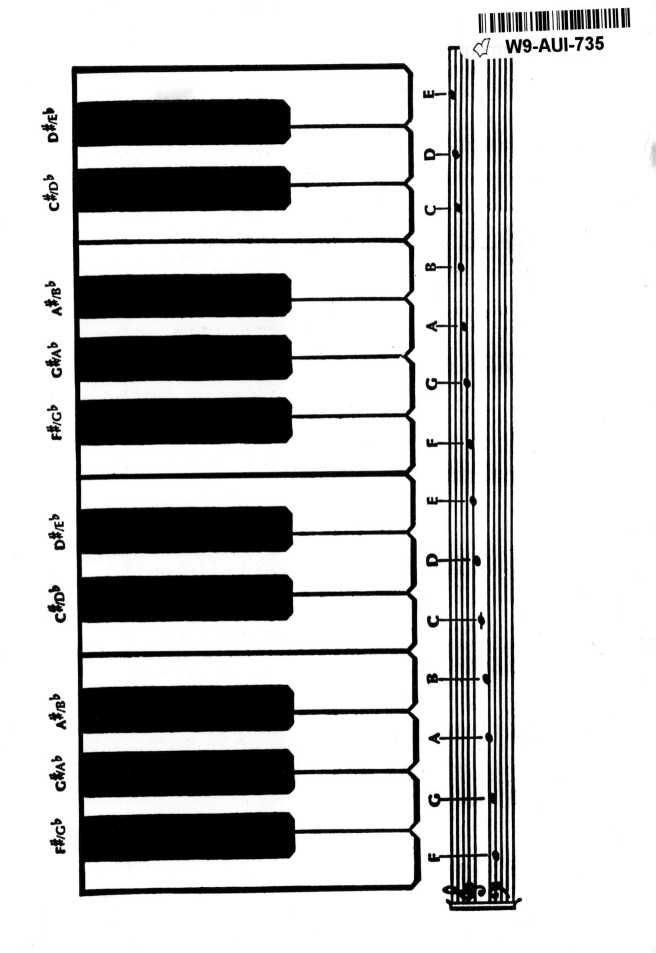

THE Music CONNECTION

PROGRAM AUTHORS

Jane Beethoven
Dulce Bohn
Patricia Shehan Campbell
Carmen E. Culp
Jennifer Davidson
Lawrence Eisman
Sandra Longoria Glover
Charlotte Hayes

Martha Hilley
Mary E. Hoffman
Hunter March
Bill McCloud
Marvelene Moore
Catherine Nadon-Gabrion
Mary Palmer
Carmino Ravosa

Mary Louise Reilly
Will Schmid
Carol Scott-Kassner
Jean Sinor
Sandra Stauffer
Judith Thomas

RECORDING PRODUCERS

Darrell Bledsoe
Jeanine Levenson

J. Douglas Pummill
Buryl Red, Executive Producer

Linda Twine
Ted Wilson

SILVER BURDETT GINN

PARSIPPANY, NJ   NEEDHAM, MA

Atlanta, GA   Deerfield, IL   Irving, TX   San Jose, CA

ISBN 0-382-26185-2

4 5 6 7 8 9 -VH- 99 98 97 96 95

C · O · N · T

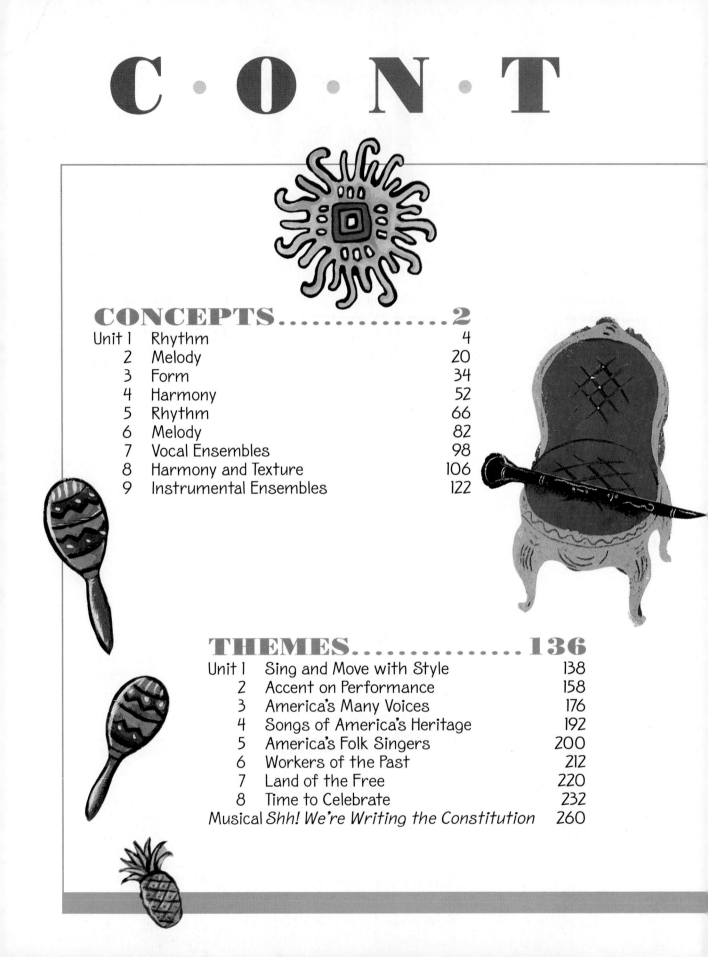

CONCEPTS............2

THEMES............136

· E · N · T · S

CONCEPTS

Do you know what makes one piece of music
sound different from another?

Is it the melody and the rhythm?

Is it the harmony or the tone color?

Rhythm, melody, form, harmony, and tone color
are the basic building blocks of music.
They are music *concepts*.

Come along and explore music concepts through
songs, instrumental parts,
listening pieces, poems, dances,
and much more.

Make the CONCEPT connection.

RAP-POETRY

Notice the words and move to the beat
as you listen to "Think Positive."

Think Positive

Words and Music by James McBride

For solo and chorus; chorus sings words in bold print.
Every single person has a different **style**,
To get to know them may take **a while**.
Love your neighbor,
Put your fears on the shelf.
If you want a better world,
Why not start with your**self**?

You can make a change with a simple **smile**,
Shake a hand, give a grin, change your **style**.
Let's improve the world we live in today,
We can find a better way **by thinking positive!**
Refrain

REFRAIN
Chorus

Nev-er give up, push for - ward, Good things come to those who give.

Fine

You can grow and learn to live, By think-ing pos - i-tive.

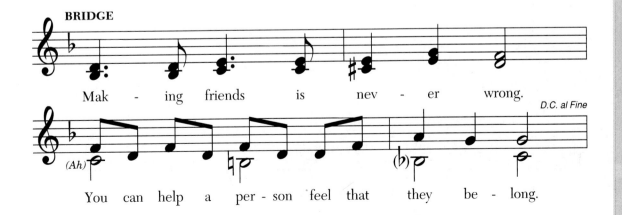

Wish, think, grow, learn, **play**,
You can make a difference every **day**.
It's a huge world filled with possibility,
It's there for you, so use your **ability**.
To make a friend, or help someone **new**,
Always let your goodness come shining **through**.
It pays to be good and it pays to be kind,
Spread peace and true friends you'll **find**.
Refrain, Bridge, Refrain

BRIDGE

Mak - ing friends is nev - er wrong.

D.C. al Fine

(Ah) You can help a per - son feel that they be - long.

It's simple like math,
Like two plus **two**.
If you do good things, good will come to **you**.
You can help a person feel good and strong
By lending a hand and helping them **along**.

A person has feelings no matter how **small**
Or big or fat or thin, or **tall**.
Never judge another, keep an open mind,
The one who is loved is the one who is **kind**.
Refrain

Coda
Give me a p, **Give me a p**.
Give me an o, **Give me an o**.
Give me an s, **Give me an s**.
What do you have? **Where's the rest?**
Think positive! **Think positive!** (*2 times*)
Think, **Think** (*4 times*)
Think positive! (*6 times*)

Find a way to show the strong steady beat as you listen to this popular piece.

The Pacifier ....Elton John

METER IN 2

In this Mexican song, a young soldier sings about his feelings for the beautiful, green-eyed Adelita.

Can you conduct the **meter** in 2?

Adelita

English Words by Aura Kontra   Folk Song from Mexico

She is known as the young A - de - li - ta,
A - de - li - ta se lla - ma la jo - ven,

And she's the one that I love and can't for - get.
A quien yo quie - ro y no pue - do ol - vi - dar.

Like the ro - ses that bloom in the mea - dow,
Y en el cam - po yo ten - go u - na ro - sa,

Oh she's the lov - li - est girl that I've met.
Y con el tiem - po la voy a cor - tar,

How I wish that she'd mar-ry this young sol-dier. __
Si A - de - li - ta qui - sie - ra ser mi es - po - sa __

__ How I wish A - de - li - ta were mine. __
__ *Si A - de - li - ta fue - ra mi mu - jer.*

__ Then I would buy her a gown of silk and sat - in, __
__ *Le com - pra - rí a un ves - ti - do de se - da,* __

__ And she would dance through the night at my side.
__ *Pa - ra lle - var - la a bai - lar al cuar - tel.*

El tilingo lingo is a song from the Mexican state of Veracruz. It is in the *jarocho* (ha ROH choh) style. Listen carefully for one of the characteristics of the *jarocho* style—the rhythmic "clicking" sounds. Are the clicks made by a percussion instrument?

As you listen, feel the meter in 2 by conducting or tapping your toes.

El tilingo lingo ....
Folk Song from Mexico

Meter in 3

Feel meter in 3 as you sing this song about the great Columbia River.

One of the verses in this song mentions six other rivers of the Northwest. What are their names? Can you find them on a map?

Roll On, Columbia

Words by Woody Guthrie   *Music Based on "Goodnight, Irene" by Huddie Ledbetter and John A. Lomax*

1. Green Doug - las   fir   where the   wa - ters   cut through,
2. Oth - er   big   ri - vers add __ pow - er   to   you,
3. At Bonne - ville   now   there are   ships   in   the locks,   The
4. And on up   the   ri - ver is the   Grand Cou - lee   Dam,   The

Down her   wild   moun - tains   and   can - yons   she   flew,   Ca -
Yak - i - ma,   Snake, and   the   Klick - i - tat,   too.
wa - ter   has   ris - en   and   cov - ered   the   rocks.
big - gest   thing   built   by   the   hand   of   a   man,   To

na - di - an   North - west   to the   o - cean   so   blue,
Sand - y,   Wil - lam - ette, and the   Hood Riv - er   too,
Ship - loads   a - plen - ty   are __ soon   past   the   docks,
run   the   great   fac' - tries   and __ wa - ter   the   land,

Roll   on,   Co - lum - bia,   roll   on. _____

Roll on, _____ Co - lum - bia, roll on. Roll on, _____ Co -

lum - bia, roll on. Your pow - er is turn - ing our

dark-ness to dawn, Roll on, Co - lum - bia, roll on. _____

Conduct meter in 3 as you listen to this piece by Erik Satie.

Gymnopedie, No.1 .... Erik Satie

A Mexican American Favorite

"De colores" tells about the beauty that can be found in the simple things of life—fields in spring colors, brightly colored birds that come from other regions, a rainbow that splashes its colors across the sky.

Follow the score as you listen to the song.

De colores

English Words by Alice Firgau   *Folk Song from Mexico*

De _____ co - lo - res, _____ De co - lo - res se vis - ten los
When _____ the mead-ows, _____ when the mead-ows burst forth in the

cam - pos en la pri - ma - ve - ra, _____
cool dew - y col - ors of spring-time; _____

De _____ co - lo - res, _____ De co - lo - res son los pa - ja -
When _____ the swal - lows, _____ when the swal-lows come wing-ing in

ri - tos que vie - nen de a - fue - ra, _____
clouds of bright col - ors from far - off; _____

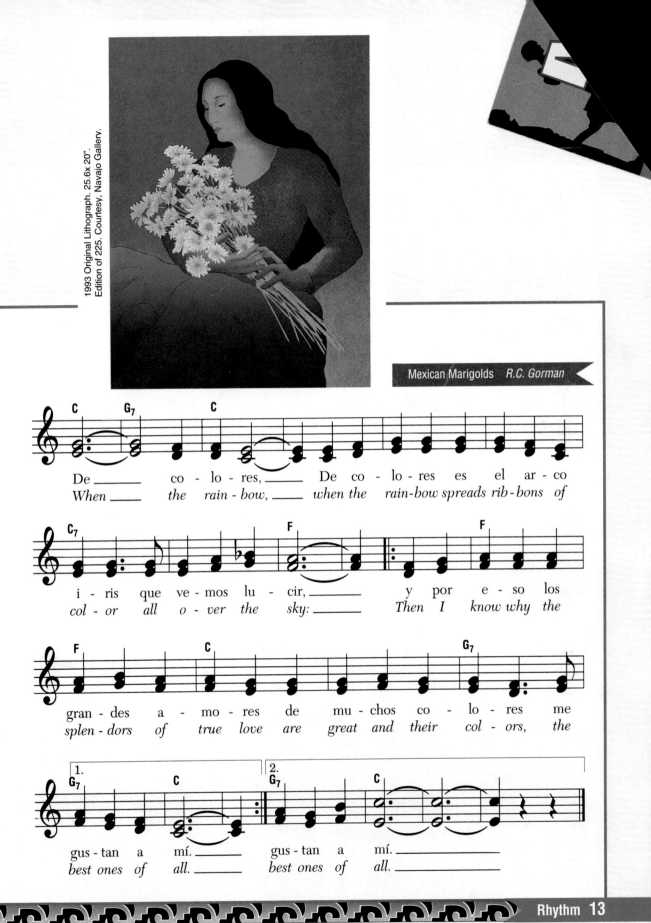

Mexican Marigolds   *R.C. Gorman*

De ___ co - lo - res, ___ De co - lo - res es el ar - co
When ___ the rain - bow, ___ when the rain-bow spreads rib-bons of

i - ris que ve - mos lu - cir, ___ y por e - so los
col - or all o - ver the sky: ___ Then I know why the

gran - des a - mo - res de mu - chos co - lo - res me
splen - dors of true love are great and their col - ors, the

1.
gus - tan a mí. ___
best ones of all. ___

2.
gus - tan a mí. ___
best ones of all. ___

METER IN 4

Tzena, Tzena

English Words by Phyllis Resnick   *Original Melody Folk Song from Israel
Collected, Compiled, and Arranged by Issachar Miron and Julius Grossman*

Tze - na, tze - na, tze - na, tze - na, come in-to the fields and we'll be -

gin ____ to work the land.   Hoe-ing, sow-ing, new things grow-ing,

pi - o-neer-ing all to-geth-er, come ____ and lend a hand.

Tze - na, tze - na, build - ing a new na - tion,

toil - ing bus - i - ly all day. _____ Soon we'll dance and

have a cel - e - bra-tion, But first we'll work and then we'll play.

Tze - na, tze - na, (clap) Tze - na, tze - na, tze - na, Tze - na, tze - na,

Tze - na, tze - na, tze - na, tze - na, Tze - na, tze - na,

(clap) Tze - na, tze-na, tze-na, Tze - na, tze - na, Tze-na, tze-na, tze-na.

AN AFRICAN AMERICAN SPIRITUAL

During the civil rights movement, many different versions of this song were sung to encourage African Americans to fight for their rights.

As you sing this song, feel the energy of the spiritual by swaying and adding a clapping pattern.

Come and Go with Me to That Land

African American Spiritual

1. Come and go with me to that land, ___
2. There's ___ no suf - f'ring in that land, ___
3. Peace ___ and free - dom in that land, ___

Come and go with me to that land, ___
There's ___ no suf - f'ring in that land, ___
Peace ___ and free - dom in that land, ___

Come and go ___ with me to that land ___ where I'm bound. ___
There's ___ no ___ suf - f'ring in that land ___ where I'm bound. ___
Peace ___ and ___ free - dom in that land ___ where I'm bound. ___

___ Come and go with me to that land, ___
___ There's ___ no suf - f'ring in that land, ___
___ Peace ___ and free - dom in that land, ___

Come and go with me to that land, ___
There's ___ no suf - f'ring in that land, ___
Peace ___ and free - dom in that land, ___

Come and go with me to that land ___ where I'm bound. ___
There's ___ no suf-f'ring in that land ___ where I'm bound. ___
Peace ___ and free-dom in that land ___ where I'm bound. ___

A Dance for Orchestra

In 1878, Antonín Dvořák wrote a group of Slavonic dances. The dances capture the feeling of Czechoslovakian folk music, but the melodies are original. They were first written as piano duets; later, Dvořák arranged them for **orchestra**. Since the *Slavonic Dances* were first played, people all over the world have enjoyed them.

Slavonic Dances, Op. 46, No. 8
.................Antonín Dvořák

As you listen to the *Slavonic Dance*, notice this rhythm pattern. It is repeated many times. Try clapping the pattern after you hear the recording.

As you listen again, notice these themes. How do they differ?

Opening Theme

Contrasting Theme

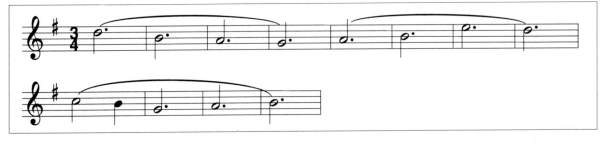

MEET THE COMPOSER

Antonín Dvořák (1841–1904)

Antonín Dvořák was born in 1841 in a small town near Prague, Czechoslovakia. His parents wanted him to become a butcher like his father. However, when young Antonín started taking violin lessons from the local schoolmaster, the course of his life changed.

Although Dvořák was sent off to learn how to become a butcher, he soon left his job and went to Prague, where he entered a music school. He later played viola in an orchestra and became one of Czechoslovakia's most famous composers.

Dvořák came to the United States in 1892 and stayed until 1895. During that time, he was head of a music conservatory. He also traveled throughout the United States and spent a summer in a Czech community in Spillville, Iowa, where his visit is still celebrated. It was while Dvořák was in the United States that he wrote his most famous work, a symphony, *From the New World.*

MELODY

A LINE OF
SOUNDS

A **melody** is a line of single tones that moves upward and downward by
step or by **leap**. Melody tones can also **repeat**.

How tones move, combined with rhythm, makes one melody different from
another. Here are three examples from songs in your book. Each one
shows how tones can move.

Steps

1.

Leaps

2.

Repeats

3.

Follow the music on the next page as you listen and identify how the tones
move in each color box.

There's Just Something About a Song

Words and Music by Janet and Ted Wilson

There's just some-thing a - bout ____ a song ____ that seems to make ev - 'ry-thing bet-ter, There's just some-thing a - bout ____ a song ____ that's es - pe-cial-ly spe - cial when we sing to-geth-er. Ev-'ry-bod-y's got a song to sing, _ So come on, let the raft - ers ring _ with a song. There's just some-thing a - bout ____ a song. song.

It does-n't mat-ter who you are, _ There's a song just right for you. _ You can make a mel - o - dy in your heart _ in ev - 'ry - thing you do. ____

STEPS, LEAPS, OR REPEATS?

In the music examples below, some notes are set off in brackets.
How do these notes move?

Try to play each of the examples on a melody instrument. Pay particular attention to the *sound* of the pattern when you play the notes in the brackets.

Listen to the song on the next page. Does the melody move mostly by steps, leaps, or repeats?

For Children Safe and Strong

Words and Music by James A. Forbes, Jr.   *Arranged by Joseph Joubert*

1. We shall o-ver-come has got to be more than a free-dom song. _ It's
2. We shall o-ver-come has got to be more than a mem-o-ry. ___ It's a
3. We shall o-ver-come has got to be more than a pro-test song. _ It's a

join-ing hands _ a-cross the land _ for chil-dren safe _ and strong. _
new re-solve _ to get in-volved _ in build-ing com-mu-ni-ty. ____
lov-ing vow _ to learn some-how _ we all can get _ a-long. _

We shall o-ver-come has got to be more than a fer-vent prayer. _ It's
We shall o-ver-come has got to be more than a dis-tant dream. _ It's
We shall o-ver-come has got to be more than a res-cue plan. _ It's a

sac-ri-fice _ at an-y price ___ to show them that ___ we care. _
hous-ing, health, _ and jobs right now, _ and a place on the free-dom team. _
wake-up call _ to one and all. ____ It's time to hope _ a-gain. _

REFRAIN

Oh, _____ there's a place for ev-'ry-one _ let us face the ris-ing sun. _

_ Then we shall o-ver-come. _____

A GARDEN OF PEOPLE

САД ЛЮДЕЙ

Follow the words as you listen to
this folk song from Russia. What do you think
"garden round the earth" means?

Garden of the Earth

English Words by Paul Winter and Paul Halley   *Traditional Song from Russia*

1. Uj ti sad ____ ti moy sad, Sad zie
   gar - den round the Earth, There's a
   voi - ces man - y tongues from the
   glo - ry of the Earth, for the

   lion - ien - ki. Ti za - chem ra - no tsve -
   home be - neath the sun, In the beau - ty of this
   moun - tains to the sea, Sing of beau - ty all a -
   glo - ry of the sun, We will sing of life to -

   1.,2.,3.   *4.*

   tiosh, ____ O - se - pa - yesh' - sia. 2. There's a
   gar - den, We will hear ____ a thou-sand songs. 3. Man - y
   round - us in this an - cient ____ har - mo - ny. 4. For the
   geth - er and for - ev - er live as one.

Listen again, and this time pay
attention to the melody. How do the
in the color boxes move?

Steps, Leaps, or Repeats?

Look through the songs listed below
and decide if the melody moves mostly
by step or mostly by leap.

- "Tzena, Tzena" (Section C), p. 14
- "Morning Has Broken," p. 26
- "Lady of the Air," p. 38
- "Away to America," p. 66
- "Blow the Wind Southerly," p. 70
- "Down Home," p. 320

CONTOUR

close
tones

The way tones move gives a melody its shape, or **contour**. How does the beginning of each phrase seem to reflect the rising of the sun?

Trace the **phrase** lines as you listen to "Morning Has Broken." Can you sing each phrase with one breath?

Morning Has Broken

Words by Eleanor Farjeon   Traditional Gaelic Melody

1. Morn - ing has bro - ken Like the first morn - ing,
2. Sweet the rain's new fall Sun - lit from heav - en,

Black - bird has spo - ken Like the first bird. _____
Like the first dew - fall On the first grass. _____

Praise for the sing - ing! Praise for the morn - ing!
Praise for the sweet - ness Of the wet gar - den,

Praise for them, spring - ing Fresh from the Word! _____
Sprung in com - plete - ness Where His feet pass. _____

© 1957 by Eleanor Farjeon. Reprinted by permission of Harold Ober Associates Inc.

AND PHRASE

The melody of "Morning Has Broken" is a traditional Gaelic (GAY lik) tune from Ireland or Scotland. On the recording, the song is accompanied by guitar and a Celtic or Irish harp similar to the one pictured in your book. Notice the sounds of this harp as you listen to the recording of "Morning Has Broken" again.

As you listen to this song from the musical comedy *The Music Man*, pay particular attention to the phrases. Are they mostly long or short?

 "Goodnight, My Someone" from
The Music Man................Meredith Willson

PHRASES and CADENCES

A Round of Goodbyes

Words and Music by Frederick Silver

Good - bye, fare - well; The time has come for part - ing.

Take care, stay well; I'll see you in a while.

We have had a lot of hap-py mem-o-ries, And I guess we've had a lot of fun;

Each phrase in this song is marked with a phrase line. When you sing the melody of "A Round of Goodbyes," you will notice that it is natural to take a breath at the end of each phrase. The ends of the phrases are called **cadences**.

A weak cadence gives an unfinished feeling, as though there is more music to come.

A strong cadence gives a feeling of coming to a resting place. The music seems finished or complete.

Trace the phrase lines above the music as you sing the song.

And I hope the mem-o-ries will lin-ger on Now that we're through and done.

Good - bye, *au re-voir, ciao,* fare thee well, We've had a hap-py time.

Good - bye, *au re-voir, ciao,* fare thee well, See you a - gain.

Listen for the cadences in this music. Are there both weak and strong cadences?

 Lobe den Herren..................German Melody

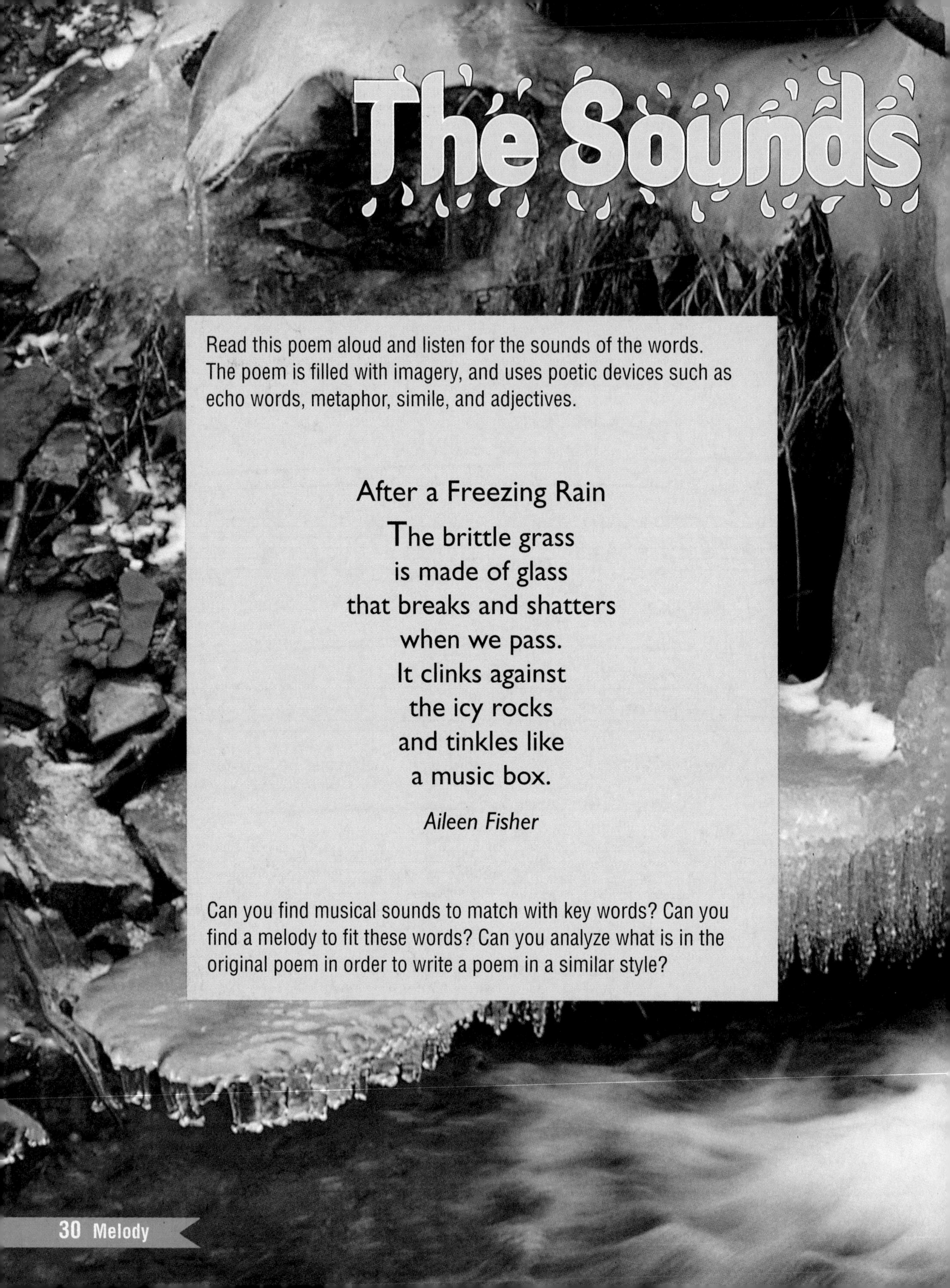

The Sounds

Read this poem aloud and listen for the sounds of the words. The poem is filled with imagery, and uses poetic devices such as echo words, metaphor, simile, and adjectives.

After a Freezing Rain

The brittle grass
is made of glass
that breaks and shatters
when we pass.
It clinks against
the icy rocks
and tinkles like
a music box.

Aileen Fisher

Can you find musical sounds to match with key words? Can you find a melody to fit these words? Can you analyze what is in the original poem in order to write a poem in a similar style?

# of Words

If you were writing a sound poem that captured the intensity of a thunderstorm, you might begin like this.

The thunder crashed
the lightning flashed
the rain upon
the rooftops splashed...

Can you finish this?

(Add percussion on x)

The   thun - der   crashed   The   light - ning flashed

The   rain   up - on   the   roof-tops splashed   *(4 beats of chimes)*

An Opera Prelude

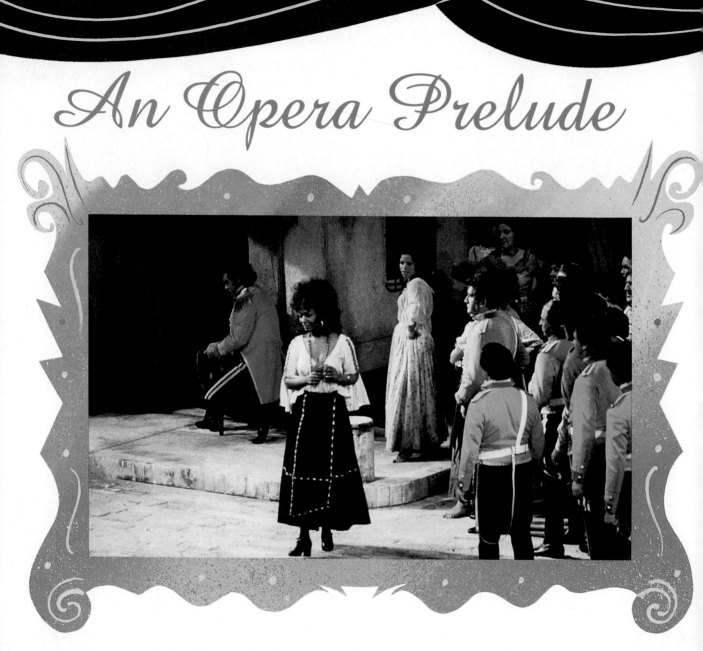

Many people think that Georges Bizet's opera *Carmen* is one of the most exciting operas ever written. Its plot is full of colorful characters—smugglers, bullfighters, soldiers, and gypsies. Before the curtain rises, the orchestra plays the "Prelude." This music sets the mood of the story.

As you listen to the "Prelude," think of a word that might describe the **mood** of the music at the beginning. Think of another word that might describe the mood of the music you hear at the end.

 "Prelude" from *Carmen*...................Georges Bizet

Here are the three main themes Bizet used in the "Prelude" to *Carmen*. You might want to listen to each **theme** before you listen to the "Prelude" again.

Themes from "Prelude" (excerpts)...............Georges Bizet

Theme 1

Theme 2

Theme 3

MEET THE COMPOSER

Georges Bizet   (1838–1875)

From early childhood, Georges Bizet showed a great interest in music; he learned the musical scale along with his alphabet. When he was nine years old, he entered the Paris Conservatory. He was an outstanding student and won many prizes for his piano playing and his compositions.

Throughout his life, Bizet was most interested in writing music for the stage. His opera *Carmen* is considered one of the great operas of all time, and today most opera houses around the world feature this popular work.

Two Sections: A and B

This song has two different sections. The letters A and B mark the beginnings of the sections. Listen to the recording and then list some differences you discovered between the sections.

Child of the Universe

Words and Music by Craig Cassils

1. The sun is on-ly a star, ___ a-round that star we spin. _
2. ⁊ Tell me, what can I aim _ for in a world that's quick-ly chang-ing?

But there are man-y oth-er stars; _ where do we fit in? ___
⁊ Tell me what my pur-pose is; ___ where do I fit in? ___

I am on-ly a grain _ of sand _ tossed by wa-ter and wind ___
Shall I fol-low a dream? _____ Or are dreams just made _ for chil-dren?

But there are man-y grains of sand; _ where do I fit in? ___
Well all of us are chil-dren now. _ That's where I fit in. ___

As we live our lives in this universe, every action we take is significant, and makes some sort of difference. This little fable illustrates the fact.

Narrator: The dove and the sparrow were talking:

Sparrow: How much do you think a snowflake weighs?

Dove: Nothing, next to nothing.

Sparrow: Then I must tell you a story. I was once caught in a storm—not the fierce, blizzard kind—rather a gentle snowstorm. And having nothing better to do, I sat on the branch of a pine tree and counted the snow flakes. I counted 3,000,000. When I got to flake 3,000,001, the branch broke off.

Narrator: So saying, the sparrow flew off, leaving the dove to think.

Dove: Perhaps then, there is but one voice waiting to be heard for peace.

B REFRAIN

Child of the u - ni - verse, Let your spi - rit fly.

You are the spe - cial one, and here's the rea - son why,

You're a child of the u - ni - verse, so climb your moun - tains high.

You are the cho - sen one to try and touch the sky.

AB or ABA form

Can you discover the meaning of *D. C. al Fine* by listening to the recording of "Jesusita"?

What is the **form** of the song?

Jesusita   *(La Jesusita)*

English Words by Aura Kontra   *Folk Song from Mexico*

Will you go danc - ing with me, how de - light - ful, _____
Va - mos al bai - le y ve - rás que bo - ni - to _____

_ Where twink-ling lights fill the air with their bright - ness. _____
_ Don - de se_a - lum - bran con vein - te lin - ter - nas. _____

_ Where those who go know the steps to the mu - sic, _____
_ Don - de se bai - lan las dan - zas mo - der - nas, _____

_ Let's join our friends as they dance the night a - way. _____

_ Don - de se bai - la de mu - cho va - ci - lón. _____

B

Be true to me Je - su - si - ta, be true to me if you please

Y quié - re - me, Je - su - si - ta, Y quié - re - me, por fa - vor;

Re - mem-ber how much I love you, my heart you must nev - er tease.

Y mi - ra que soy tu a - man - te y se - gu - ro ser - vi - dor.

This song is a musical tribute to Amelia Earhart, who is sometimes referred to as the First Lady of the Air.

Lady of the Air

Words and Music by John Carter and Mary Kay Beall

La - dy ___ of the air, my A - me - lia,

La - dy ___ of the air, my i - deal,

La - dy won't you say where you are to - day?

La - dy of the air, A - me - lia. ___

La - dy ___ of the air, my A - me - lia,

La - dy ___ of the air, my i - deal,

SECTIONS

Follow the music as you listen to "Lady of the Air." How many sections are there? What differences can you discover between the A and B sections?

La - dy won't you say where you are to - day?

La - dy of the air, A - me - lia. *(last time to Coda)*

B

1. Once in a life - time a la - dy does what no
2. Once in a life - time a la - dy flies o - ver

oth - er can do; _____ O - pen the eyes __ of the
land __ and sea; _____ Dar - ing to go ____ where _

world to see that la - dies can make dreams come true! Oh,
ev - 'ry one knows dan - ger is cer - tain to be. Oh

D.C.

Coda

A - me - lia. _____

A RHYTHMIC AFRICAN AMERICAN SPIRITUAL

The rhythm of this song has a catchy, off-balance feeling.
As you sing or listen, clap the **melodic rhythm** during
Section A and clap the **steady beat** during Section B.

Bell or Recorder Part for Section A

Ev'ry Time I Feel the Spirit

African American Spiritual

A REFRAIN

Ev - 'ry time I _____ feel the spir - it _____ mov - in'

in my heart _ I will pray; Ev - 'ry time I _____ feel the

spir - it _____ mov - in' in my heart _ I _____ will pray.

B VERSE

1. Up on the moun - tain _____ when my Lord spoke,
2. I got a home in _____ the Prom - ised Land,

Percussion Ostinatos for Section A

Which part will you play to accompany Section A of "Ev'ry Time I Feel the Spirit"?

Drum

Tambourine

Triangle

Festive Music   *Sanfa Sanu*

Out of His mouth came ____ fire and smoke,
Ain't gon - na stop till I shake His hand,

I looked a - round me, ____ It looked so fine,
Now Jor - dan riv - er ____ is chilly and cold,

D.C. al Fine

I asked my Lord if ____ all was mine.
It chills the bod - y ____ not the soul.

THREE DIFFERENT SECTIONS – RONDO FORM

A   B   A   C   A

Listen to *Help Me Rondo* to discover how the arrangement of the themes is like the art shown at the top of the page.

Help Me Rondo................Jeanine Levenson

Theme A

Theme B

Theme C

After you listen to the piece several times, make a chart on blank paper. List the musical characteristics of each theme.

Follow the chart as you listen. It will help you hear how the sections of this ragtime music are put together to create a **rondo** form.

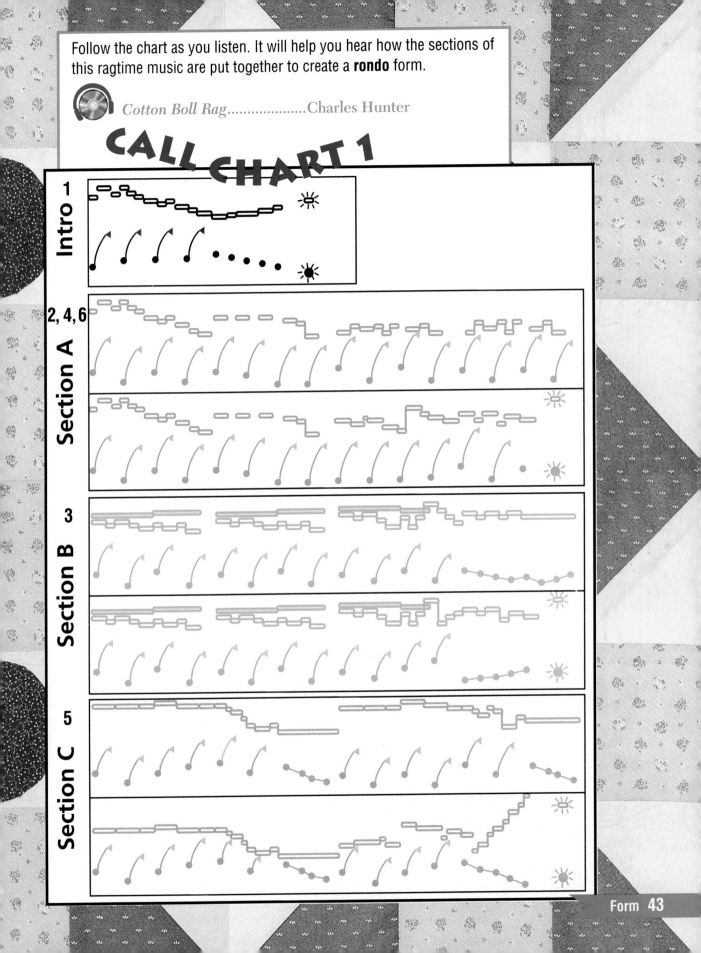

Cotton Boll Rag....................Charles Hunter

CALL CHART 1

Intro 1

Section A 2, 4, 6

Section B 3

Section C 5

Bavarian composer Carl Orff loved flowers and nature. Perhaps this enabled him to write the springtime section of his choral piece *Carmina Burana* with such beauty and energy.

 "Chramer, gip die varwe mir" from *Carmina Burana* ....Carl Orff

Below is the theme of "Chramer, gip die varwe mir" ("Shopkeeper, give me color to make up my face"). The melody is good for singing on *la* or playing on a glockenspiel or soprano metallophone. This melody is represented by the circle on page 45.

Spring

Add the following instrumental parts and play throughout.

Follow the map below as you listen to the rest of the piece. Many dance companies have choreographed *Carmina Burana*. How might you move to the different parts of this piece?

 "Tanz" ("Dance") from *Carmina Burana* ....Carl Orff

Chant the following words, clapping where they are underlined.

Spring-time　　　spring-time　　　win-ter-time

Repeat the line, but this time say *win-ter-time* twice.

Spring-time　　　spring-time　　　win-ter-time　　win-ter-time

Put it all together and repeat.

a Dance

You now have the mixed meter feel of 2 plus 3, which Orff used in "Tanz." This was very comfortable for him because he knew many Bavarian folk dances that used this kind of mixed rhythmic patterns.

For your "tanz," try long, leaping strides on the words *springtime* (two leaps). Try skipping only once in place on the word *wintertime*. Use the movement and speech patterns on the main theme parts of "Tanz."

Discover the Rondo Form of "Tanz"

Decide how you will move in the sections between the main theme. Is the music rhythmical in the same way as in the main theme or is it more free?

A   B   A   C   A

"Ecce gratum" from *Carmina Burana*
..................Carl Orff

Theme and Variations

What is the theme, or subject, of the pictures shown below?

How has the subject been changed to make each picture look different?

A Musical Theme

A familiar melody can be used as a musical theme for a set of variations.
Play this theme on a melody instrument. Do you recognize the tune?

A theme can be changed so that it sounds different. Can you think of a
way to vary, or change, the theme that you played?

On the next page you will find four variations on the familiar-tune theme.
Can you discover how the theme has been changed to make each variation
sound different?

Four Variations

In the following piece you will hear a familiar theme and variations on that theme. How has the theme been changed to make each variation sound different?

Variations on "Yankee Doodle" ....Joseph Joubert

Theme and Variations

The theme of this piece is based on "When Johnny Comes Marching Home," found on page 324 in your book. Following the chart will help you hear what is going on as the music goes along.

CALL CHART 2

American Salute .... Morton Gould

Form 51

ADDING COUNTERMELODIES

In music, **texture** has to do with the layering of sound. A melody by itself has a thin texture. When you combine melodies, the texture becomes thicker.

What happens to the texture of this song as each **countermelody** is added?

Our Melody
from the *Fraggle Rock Show*

Our mel-o-dy, come and sing it with me, it's a song where you know you be-long.

Our mel-o-dy, come and sing it with me 'cause you know we be-long to the song.

Countermelody 1

La la la la la la la la la la la la

Countermelody 2

Da da da dee da da da da da dee da da da da da dee da da da

da da da dee da da da

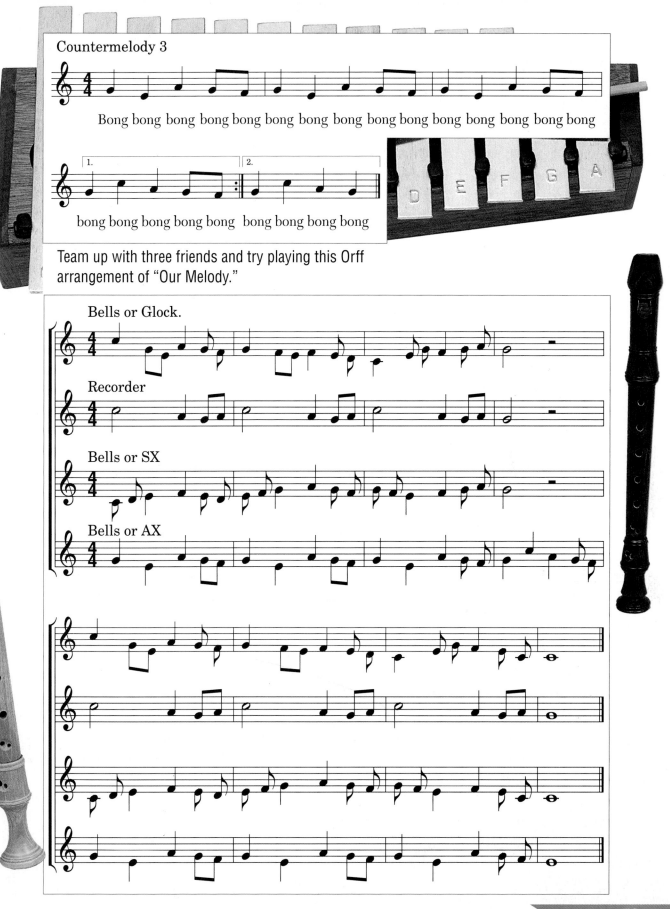

Countermelody 3

Bong bong bong bong bong bong bong bong bong bong bong bong bong bong bong

1. bong bong bong bong bong   2. bong bong bong bong

Team up with three friends and try playing this Orff arrangement of "Our Melody."

Bells or Glock.

Recorder

Bells or SX

Bells or AX

MELODY AND DESCANT

A **descant** is a kind of countermelody that is higher than the main melody of a song. You can create harmony by adding a descant to a melody. Listen for the descant in the recording of "Streets of Laredo." Is it always sung?

Streets of Laredo

Cowboy Song from the United States

Descant

1 Slow, slow, bang the drum slow,

Melody

2
1. As I _____ walked out in the streets of La - re - do,
2. "I see by your out - fit that you are a cow - boy,"
3. "Now once in the sad - dle I used to ride hand-some,
4. "Go run to the spring for a cup of cold wa - ter,
5. We'll bang the drum slow - ly and play the fife low - ly,

1 Bang the drum slow, Bang the drum slow.

2
As I walked out in La - re - do one day,
These words he said as I bold - ly walked by;
'A handsome young cow - boy' is what they would say,
To cool down my fe - ver," the young cow - boy said.
We'll play the dead march as we bear him a - long.

Some composers use folk-song melodies in their compositions. Listen for the melody of "Streets of Laredo" in this piano piece by an American composer—Roy Harris. Has the composer changed the melody?

"Streets of Laredo" from *American Ballads* ....Roy Harris

Low, low play the fife low,

I spied a young cow-boy wrapped up in white lin - en,
"Come lis - ten to me and I'll tell my sad sto - ry
I'd ride in - to town and go down to the card - house,
But when I re - turned, his poor soul had de - part - ed,
We'll go to the grave - yard and lay the sod o'er him;

Play the fife low, Oh, so low.

wrapped up in white lin - en and cold as the clay.
I'm shot in the chest and I'm sure I will die."
But I'm shot in the chest and I'm dy - ing to - day."
And I wept when I saw the young cow - boy was dead.
He was a young cow - boy, but he had done wrong.

MELODY & COUNTER MELODY

The melody and countermelody of this song from old Broadway are each written on a separate staff. Follow one of the melodies as you listen to the recording. The color boxes will help you keep your place.

Give My Regards to Broadway
from *Little Johnny Jones*

Words and Music by George M. Cohan

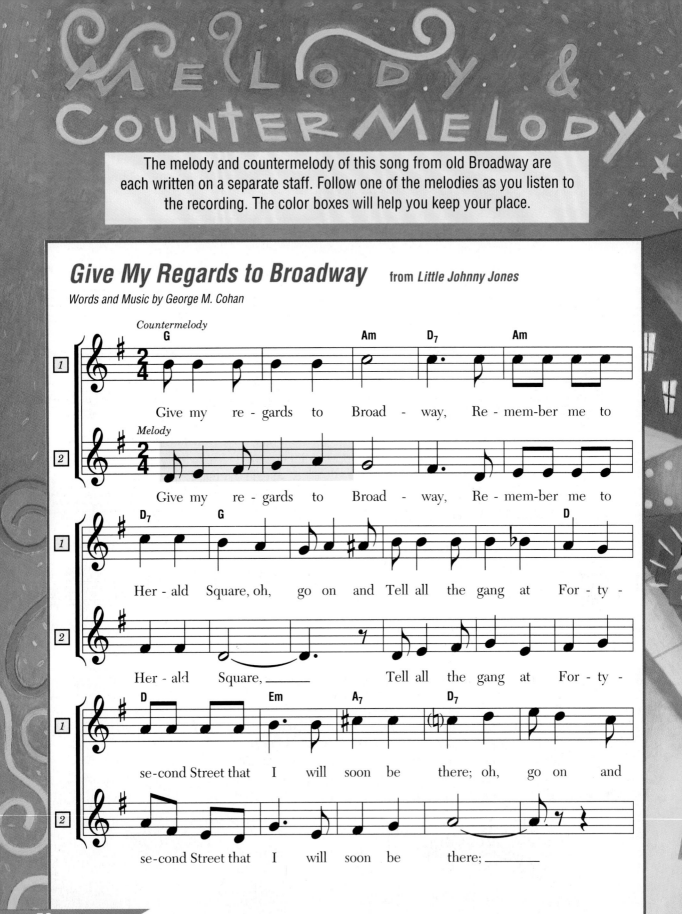

Whis-per of how I'm yearn - ing To min - gle with the

Whis-per of how I'm yearn - ing To min - gle with the

old time throng, oh, go on and Give my re - gards to old Broad -

old time throng, _____ Give my re - gards to old Broad -

way, And say that I'll be there e're long. _____

way, And say that I'll be there e're long. _____

MUSICAL

These well-known songs of the West can be sung together. Form two groups and try it. The result will be two-part **harmony**.

My Home's in Montana

Cowboy Song from the United States   *Adapted by M. Hoffman*

My home's in Mon - tan - a, I wear a ban - dan - a; My

spurs are of sil - ver, my po - ny is gray. When rid - ing the

rang - es, my luck nev-er chang-es; With foot in the stir - rup I

gal - lop a - way. Home on the roll - ing range,

That's where I want to stay! When rid - ing the rang - es my

luck nev - er chang-es; With foot in the stir-rup I gal - lop a - way.

Home On the Range

Cowboy Song from the United States

Oh, give me a home where the buf-fa-lo roam, Where the deer and the an-te-lope play;_____ Where sel-dom is heard a dis-cour-ag-ing word, And the skies are not cloud-y all day._____ Home, home on the range,_____ where the deer and the an-te-lope play;_____ Where sel-dom is heard a dis-cour-ag-ing word, And the skies are not cloud-y all day._____

CREATING HARMONY

When your class knows the melody of "Old Abram Brown,"
sing the song as a two-, three-, or four-part **round**.

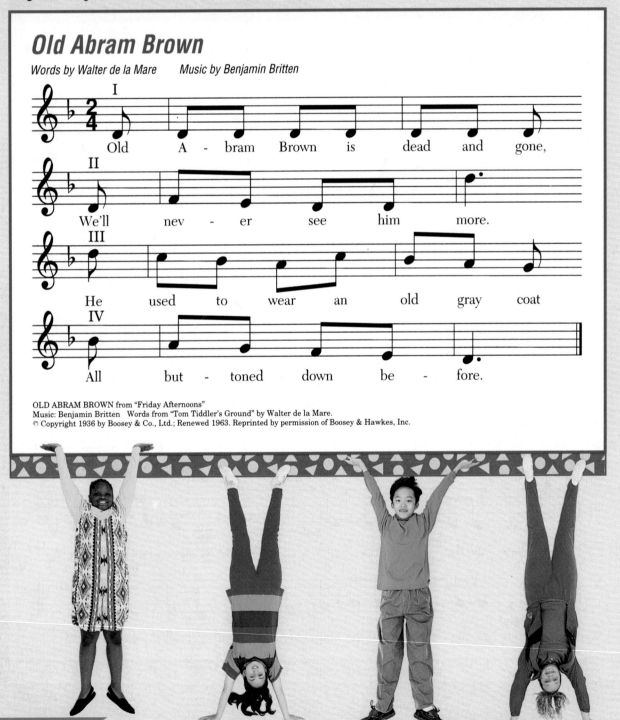

Old Abram Brown

Words by Walter de la Mare   *Music by Benjamin Britten*

I

Old   A - bram   Brown   is   dead   and   gone,

II

We'll   nev - er   see   him   more.

III

He   used   to   wear   an   old   gray   coat

IV

All   but - toned   down   be - fore.

OLD ABRAM BROWN from "Friday Afternoons"
Music: Benjamin Britten   Words from "Tom Tiddler's Ground" by Walter de la Mare.
© Copyright 1936 by Boosey & Co., Ltd.; Renewed 1963. Reprinted by permission of Boosey & Hawkes, Inc.

Mystery Melody

Compare this melody with "Old Abram Brown." Can you discover how this melody was created? There is a special musical term for this kind of writing—**retrograde.**

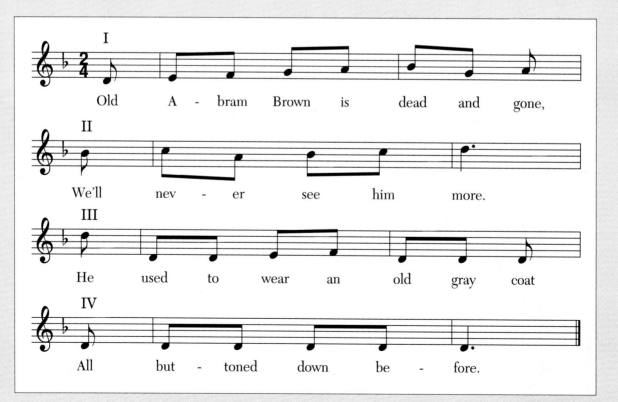

I

Old A - bram Brown is dead and gone,

II

We'll nev - er see him more.

III

He used to wear an old gray coat

IV

All but - toned down be - fore.

THREE-PART ROUND

In order to sing "Tumba" as a three-part round, you must be able to do two things well:
• Sing the melody independently.
• Keep the beat steady.

Tumba

Melody from Palestine

I
Tum-ba tum-ba tum-ba tum, Tum-ba tum-ba tum-ba tum.

II
La la la la la la, La la la la la,

La la la la la la, La la la la.

III
Tum - ba, Tum - ba, Tum - ba.

Ostinatos Choose one of these patterns to play on a mallet instrument as an **accompaniment** for "Tumba." Play throughout the song.

1.

2.

3.

A Fable

The Camel Dances .... Arnold Lobel

The Camel had her heart set on becoming a ballet dancer. "To make every movement a thing of grace and beauty," said the Camel. "That is my one and only desire."

Again and again she practiced her pirouettes, her relevés, and her arabesques. She repeated the five basic positions a hundred times each day. She worked for long months under the hot desert sun. Her feet were blistered and her body ached with fatigue, but not once did she think of stopping.

At last the Camel said, "Now I am a dancer." She announced a recital and danced before an invited group of camel friends and critics. When her dance was over, she made a deep bow. There was no applause.

"I must tell you frankly," said a member of the audience, "as a critic and a spokesperson for this group, that you are lumpy and humpy. You are baggy and bumpy. You are, like the rest of us, simply a camel. You are *not* and never will be a ballet dancer!"

Chuckling and laughing, the audience moved away across the sand. "How very wrong they are!" said the Camel. "I have worked hard. There can be no doubt that I am a splendid dancer. I will dance and dance just for myself." That is what she did. It gave her many years of pleasure.

Satisfaction will come to those who please themselves.

A COMPOSER OF TODAY

Libby Larsen wrote *Four on the Floor* in 1983. It is scored for four instruments—violin, cello, double bass, and piano. Following the call chart as you listen will help you keep track of what is happening in the music. After you listen, write a few words or phrases that describe the overall effect of the music.

CALL CHART 3

Four on the Floor ....Libby Larsen

1. Short **introduction**; piano and pizzicato strings.

2. Section 1 begins; walking bass in piano.

3. Strings join piano; walking bass in piano continues.

4. **Pizzicato** strings without piano; tempo gradually slows to end Section 1.

5. Section 2 begins; slower tempo; swinging triplet patterns; melody is more smoothly connected.

6. Dialogue between piano and strings.

7. Getting faster leading into Section 3.

8. Walking bass returns; Section 3 begins (similar to section 1).

9. Pizzicato strings; piano drops out.

10. Bowed strings; piano returns.

11. Piano and strings; strings improvise runs and **glissandos**.

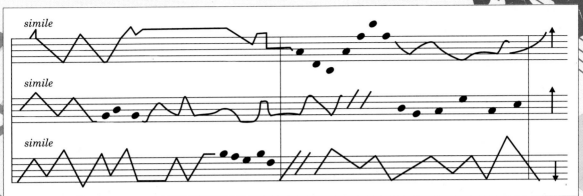

12. Coda begins; strings and piano, sometimes alone and sometimes together, race ahead to the end.

MEET THE COMPOSER

Libby Larsen

(1950–   )

Libby Larsen, one of America's most celebrated living composers, was born in Wilmington, Delaware. Her many compositions include works for orchestra, theater, opera, ballet, and chamber groups. Well-known conductors, orchestras, and soloists perform her music throughout the United States and Europe in concert halls and at music festivals. Energy, rhythmic excitement, and imagination fill her music.

Libby Larsen has received many awards. She also works hard for the advancement of today's music and musicians.

METER IN 6

Away to America

Words and Music by Linda Williams

Dm   G   C   Dm   Am

1. My grand-fa-ther jour-neyed, like so man-y oth-ers, He turned to the West and the
heard of the moun-tains in far Col-o - ra-do, Where ea-gles flew free in the

all he took with him was what he could car-ry, His books and an old vi-o-
moth-er was born there not man-y years af-ter, And all of her sis-ters as

Dm   G   C

sun. ___ He sailed out of Bris - tol a - long with his broth-ers, A
air. ___ He'd find a high moun-tain and live in its sha-dow, For
lin. ___ Wait-ing to meet him: a girl he would mar - ry, A
well, ___ And all of the years, all the tears and the laugh-ter, Are

1. Dm   Am   Dm   **2.** Dm   G₇   C₇

new world was there to be won.   He'd some-thing was call-ing him there. __
new life a - bout to be - gin.   My there in the stor-ies they tell. __

The writer of this song tells a true story. It was her grandfather who sailed to America. All the places exist, and the events in the song really happened.

Feel six **beats** to a measure as you listen to the recording.

REFRAIN

F   Am   B♭   C₇   F   Am   B♭   F

"Sail a - way,   a - way to A - mer - i - ca,   Far   off   o - ver the sea.

Dm   Gm   F   Gm   C₇   Dm   D.S.

There is some-thing there in A-mer-i-ca,   And it's call-ing to me."   2. Now

3. Now I've gone away, there was nothing to hold me,
    I flew off to London and stayed.
    But still I remember the stories they told me,
    And think of the journey he made.
    Now I miss the mountains when I look around me,
    And I really can't tell you when,
    But somehow the voice of my grandfather found me
    And soon I'll be flying again.
    Fly away, come home to America . . .

    (Repeat Refrain) Sail away . . .

Listen to another song about coming to America. Can you discover some similarities and differences between this song and "Away to America?"

 "America" from *The Jazz Singer* ....Neil Diamond

Conducting Patterns for Meter in 6

In $\frac{6}{8}$ meter the **strong beat** is the first of a group of six steady beats. Clap beats in sets of six. Make the first beat in each set stronger than the others.

A conductor uses this pattern for meter in 6. Try it. Think *1 2 3 4 5 6* as you make the motions.

Use the conducting pattern to keep time to this music that moves in a slow $\frac{6}{8}$ meter.

On Hearing the First Cuckoo in Spring (excerpt) ....Frederick Delius

Tempo Makes a Difference

When music written in $\frac{6}{8}$ meter is performed at a fast **tempo**, the conductor feels the music moving in twos and shows only the first and fourth beats.

1 2 3 **4** 5 6   **1** 2 3 **4** 5 6

Try conducting this music. It moves in a fast $\frac{6}{8}$ meter.

 "Allegro Finale" from *Sonata in F*
.................George Frideric Handel

Practice Conducting

You can practice the conducting patterns for $\frac{6}{8}$ meter with these songs from your book. Listen to the recording and then decide whether to use a conducting pattern in 6 or in 2.

- "Viva Jujuy," p. 72
- "Seventy Six Trombones," p. 88
- "Lift Ev'ry Voice and Sing," p. 228
- "Stars of the Heavens," p. 319
- "The Derby Ram," p. 322
- "When Johnny Comes Marching Home," p. 324
- "Paddy Works on the Railway," p. 326

THE RHYTHM OF THE SEA

This old folk song from the northernmost county of England tells about the long and lonely wait for a sailor's return from the sea.

Feel the gentle rocking motion of meter in 6 as you listen to this song of the sea. Which $\frac{6}{8}$ conducting pattern will you use?

🎧 *Long Trip* ....Langston Hughes

Long Trip

The sea is a wilderness of
    waves,
A desert of water.
We dip and dive,
Rise and roll,
Hide and are hidden
On the sea,
    Day, night,
    Night, day,
The sea is a desert of waves,
A wilderness of water.

Langston Hughes

Blow the Wind Southerly

Folk Song from Northumbria

Blow the wind south-er-ly, south-er-ly, south-er-ly,

Blow the wind south o'er the bon-ny blue sea;

Blow the wind south-er-ly, south-er-ly, south-er-ly,

Blow bon-ny breeze __ my true love to me.

The Fog Warning 1885 *Winslow Homer*

B

F C7 F C7

1. He told me last night there were ships in the off - ing, And
2. I stood by the light-house that last time we part - ed, Till

F C G7 C

    I hur - ried down to the deep roll - ing sea; But my
dark - ness came down o'er the deep roll - ing sea; And no

B♭ F C7 F

eye could not see it, wher - ev - er might be it, The
long - er I saw the bright bark of my true ___ love,

F B♭ C7 F   *D.C. al Fine*

bark that is bear - ing my true love to me.
Blow bon - ny breeze ___ and bring him to me.

A song from Argentina

"Viva Jujuy" is a love song, but not a love song written for a person. It is a song of love for one's home. *Jujuy* is the name of a province in Argentina that is in an area called *Humahuaqueña.*

Viva Jujuy

English Words by Aura Kontra   *Folk Song from Argentina*

Long live Ju - juy, ___ long live the high land,   Long live my true love.
Vi - va Ju - juy, ___ vi - va la pu - na,   Vi - va mi a - ma - da.

Long live the can-yon   and loft - y moun-tains   Soar-ing high a - bove.
Vi - van los ce - rros   pin - ta ra - jea - dos   De mi que - bra - da.

Soar - ing high a - bove   Hu - ma - hua - que - ña.
De mi que - bra - da   Hu - ma - hua - que - ña.

I'll nev-er leave you.   I'll not for-sake you.   I be-long to you.
No te se - pa - res   De mis a - mo - res   Tu e - res mi due - ña.

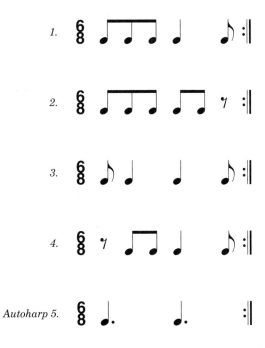

Estancia was written for a dance company.
What element of music is most noticeable?

Estancia, Movement 1
..............Alberto Ginastera

EVEN AND UNEVEN

Follow the music as you listen to "Scotland the Brave." The combination of the steady beat and the uneven melodic rhythm adds spirit to this patriotic song from Scotland.

What instruments do you hear in this recording of Scottish folk music?

 The Sounds of Scotland ....Traditional

Scotland the Brave

Words by Cliff Hanley   *Traditional Tune from Scotland*

Hark, when the night is fall-ing, Hear! Hear the pipes are call-ing,

Loud-ly and proud-ly call-ing, down through the glen.

There, where the hills are sleep-ing, now feel the blood a-leap-ing,

High as the spir-its of the old High-land men.

REFRAIN

Tower-ing in gal-lant fame, Scot-land my moun-tain hame,

Add a Part

Here is a percussion part to play as an accompaniment for
Brave." Play it all through the song.

Drum

High may your proud stan-dards glo - rious-ly wave for-ev-er.

Land of my high en-deav-or, Land of the shin-ing riv-er,

Land of my heart for-ev-er, Scot-land the brave.

DOTTED RHYTHM

at important things can one good friend offer to another? Pete Seeger offers this song as a gift to his friends everywhere.

As you learn this song, notice that some of the rhythms in the melody are even and some are uneven. Can you feel the difference between even and uneven rhythms?

Do a tap-snap pattern as you listen to "Precious Friends." Try this one, and then make up your own pattern.

(tap   snap   tap   snap)

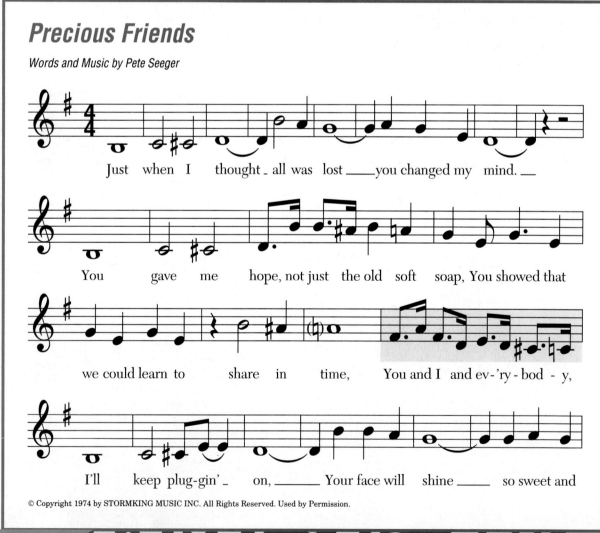

Precious Friends

Words and Music by Pete Seeger

Just when I thought all was lost ___ you changed my mind. ___

You gave me hope, not just the old soft soap, You showed that

we could learn to share in time, You and I and ev-'ry-bod-y,

I'll keep plug-gin' on, ___ Your face will shine ___ so sweet and

Listen to the recording of this spiritual and identify
the phrases that have uneven rhythm patterns.

Keep in the Middle of the Road

African American Spritual

1. I hear them an-gels call-in' loud,
2. I have no time to stop an' talk, Keep in the mid-dle of the
3. The world is full of sin-ful things,

They are wait-in' there in a great big crowd,
road, 'Cause the road is rough an' it's hard to walk,
When your feet get tired put ___ on your wings,

Keep in the mid-dle of the road.
I can see them stand-in' 'round the
Gon - na fix my eyes ___ on the
When you lay down in ___ that ___

big white gate, Gon-na trav-el a - long ___ be-fore it gets too late, For it
gold-en stair, Gon-na keep ___ on a - go-in' 'til ___ I get there, For my
road to die, Watch ___ them ___ an - gels ___ in the sky, Put ___

Plantation Scene
Artist Unknown

Chorus

ain't no use for to sit down, and wait,
head is bound that __ crown for to wear, Keep in the mid-dle of the road. __
on your wings and __ get up an' fly,

B **REFRAIN**

So chil-dren keep in the mid-dle of the road, Chil-dren keep in the

mid - dle of the road, Don't you look to the right, don't you

look to the left, Just keep in the mid - dle of the road.

AN AMERICAN

The music you will hear is from Leonard Bernstein's *Mass*—a theater piece for singers, players, and dancers. Bernstein created the work for the opening of the John F. Kennedy Center for the Performing Arts in Washington, D.C., in 1971.

As you listen to the recording, think about what is going on in the music. Listen especially for the strong rhythmic accents and the solo-chorus, or call-and-response, style.

 "Gloria Tibi" from *Mass* ....Leonard Bernstein

An Unusual Meter

One of the elements that makes Bernstein's "Gloria Tibi" so exciting is the strong, driving rhythm that is heard and felt from the beginning of the piece to the very end.

COMPOSER

Look at the **rhythm pattern** notated below. What does the **meter signature** tell you? Try tapping or clapping the pattern along with the bongo part as you listen to "Gloria Tibi" again.

MEET THE COMPOSER

Leonard Bernstein

(1918–1990)

Leonard Bernstein was born in Lawrence, Massachusetts. He attended Harvard University and the Curtis Institute of Music. He continued his musical education at Tanglewood (home of the Berkshire Music Festival) during the summers of 1940–1942. When Bernstein was a young man of 25, he was appointed assistant conductor of the New York Philharmonic. He became famous overnight when he filled in for a conductor who was suddenly taken ill. In 1958, Bernstein became the first American-born conductor to be appointed director of the New York Philharmonic—one of the greatest orchestras in the world.

A PENTATONIC

Lahk gei mohlee

Folk Song from Taiwan

六　月　茉　莉　真　正　美
Lahk　gei＿　moh　lee＿　jeen　jeeahn＿　shwee,

郎　君　生　著　你　都　真　古　椎
long　goon＿　sheen　jway　lee　go　jeen＿　go　jwee.

好　花　難　得　成　雙　對
Hoh　hway　lahn＿　dee＿　sheen＿　shiong＿　dwee,

身　邊　哪　没　娘　啊　你　都　上　刻　虧
sheen　bean　nah　moh　new ah　lee - goh　shiong＿　keh＿　kwee.

Jasmine Flowers of June

Words by Hsu Ping-Ting   Transliterated by Han Kuo-Huang   Adapted by Rebecca Schwann
Folk Song from Taiwan

1. White jas-mine flow-ers of the Sixth Moon are fair,
2. White jas-mine flow-ers of the Sixth Moon are fair,
3. White jas-mine flow-ers of the Sixth Moon are fair,

And there's a young lad who's no-ble and fine.
Love-ly____ lass____ has nev-er been found.
Lass-es a-lone____ are sor-ry and sad.

Love-ly flow-ers rare-ly ev-er grow__ all a-lone;
Flowers and lass-es should nev-er be____ a-lone;
Love-ly flow-ers should be bloom-ing side__ by___ side.

Fair lone-ly lass can__ be ____ sad, _____ so _____ sad.
Sad is the love-ly__ lass who's nev-er,__ nev-er__ found.
When will the lass be __found and nev-er__ be_ a-lone?

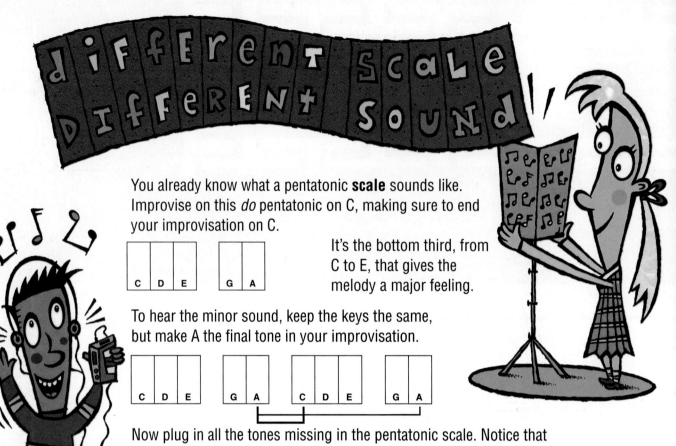

Different Scale Different Sound

You already know what a pentatonic **scale** sounds like. Improvise on this *do* pentatonic on C, making sure to end your improvisation on C.

C	D	E		G	A

It's the bottom third, from C to E, that gives the melody a major feeling.

To hear the minor sound, keep the keys the same, but make A the final tone in your improvisation.

C	D	E		G	A		C	D	E		G	A

Now plug in all the tones missing in the pentatonic scale. Notice that it is the third that gives the scale its unique major or minor sound.

MAJOR

C	D	E	F	G	A	B	C

MINOR

A	B	C	D	E	F	G	A

Sing and play the canon below. Notice how many times the E is used, reinforcing the major sound.

Alleluia, Amen   (Version One)

Traditional Round

I. C   F   C   F   G7   C
Al - le - lu - ia,   al - le - lu - ia,

II. C   F   C   F   G7   C
A -   men,   a -   men.

Play the canon from A to A to hear it in a minor variation.
Notice how many times the C is used, reinforcing the minor sound.

minor 3rd

If you make "Alleluia, Amen" minor starting on C,
you must add **accidentals** to make the scale correct.

Alleluia, Amen   (Version Two)

Traditional Round

I

Al - le - lu - ia,   al - le - lu - ia,

II

A - men,   a - men.

Let's look at this another way.

Find a keyboard and play the major
third—C to E.

Now make the third smaller by moving
one-half step lower, from E to E♭. You
just played a minor third.

Play all the keys, white and black, from C to C.
You just played a **chromatic scale** by playing
all the **half steps**. Now play **whole steps**.

Can you now figure out the pattern
for a **major scale**?

C D E F G A B C
W W H W W W H

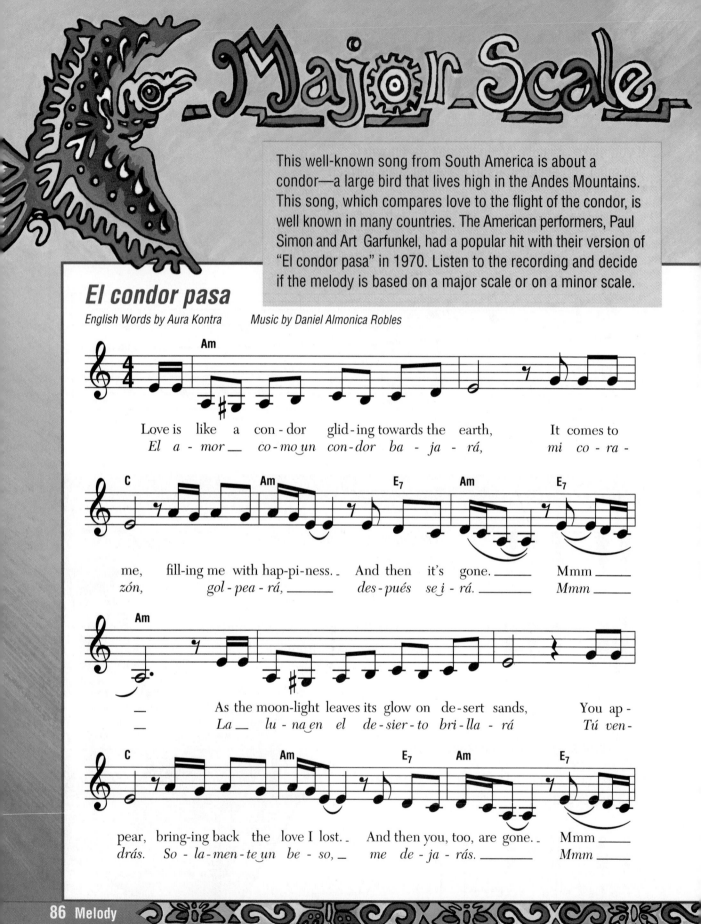

Major Scale

This well-known song from South America is about a condor—a large bird that lives high in the Andes Mountains. This song, which compares love to the flight of the condor, is well known in many countries. The American performers, Paul Simon and Art Garfunkel, had a popular hit with their version of "El condor pasa" in 1970. Listen to the recording and decide if the melody is based on a major scale or on a minor scale.

El condor pasa

English Words by Aura Kontra   *Music by Daniel Almonica Robles*

Love is   like   a   con - dor   glid - ing towards the   earth,   It comes to
El   a - mor __   co - mo un   con - dor   ba - ja - rá,   mi   co - ra -

me,   fill - ing me with hap - pi - ness..   And then   it's   gone. ____   Mmm ____
zón,   gol - pea - rá, _____   des - pués se i - rá. _____   Mmm ____

_   As the moon - light leaves its glow on de - sert sands,   You ap -
_   La __   lu - na en el   de - sier - to bri - lla - rá   Tú ven -

pear,   bring - ing back   the   love I lost. _   And then you, too, are gone. _   Mmm ____
drás.   So - la - men - te un be - so, _   me de - ja - rás. _____   Mmm ____

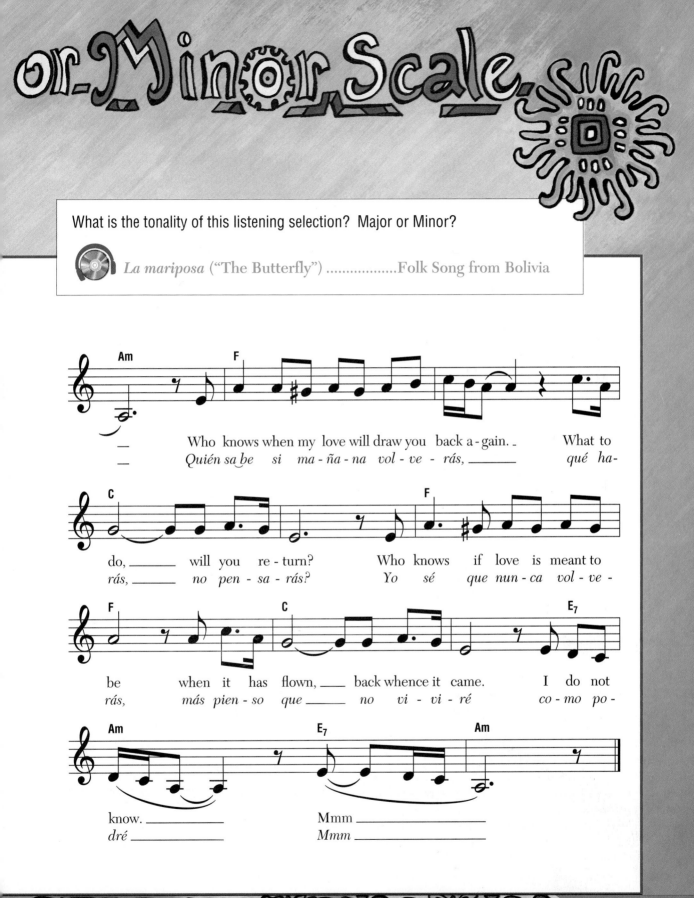

What is the tonality of this listening selection? Major or Minor?

La mariposa ("The Butterfly") ....Folk Song from Bolivia

Who knows when my love will draw you back a-gain. What to
Quién sa be si ma-ña-na vol-ve-rás, _____ qué ha-

do, _____ will you re-turn? Who knows if love is meant to
rás, _____ no pen-sa-rás? Yo sé que nun-ca vol-ve-

be when it has flown, ___ back whence it came. I do not
rás, más pien-so que _____ no vi-vi-ré co-mo po-

know. _____ Mmm _____
dré _____ Mmm _____

major or minor

Seventy Six Trombones

from *The Music Man*   *Words and Music by Meredith Willson*

> Listen to this well-known song from *The Music Man*. Is it based on a major or minor scale?

A *Solo*

Sev - en - ty   six   trom - bones   led   the   big   pa - rade, __
          six   trom - bones   caught   the   morn - ing   sun, __

__ With   a   hun-dred and   ten   cor - nets   close   at   hand. ____
__ With   a   hun-dred and   ten   cor - nets   right   be - hind. ____

__ They   were   fol - lowed by   rows   and   rows   of   the   fin - est   vir - tu -
__ There were   more than   a   thou - sand   reeds spring-ing   up ___   like ___

1.
o - sos,   The cream   of   ev - 'ry   fa - mous   band. ____   Sev - en - ty
weeds, There were horns   of

2.
ev - 'ry shape   and   kind. ____   There were

B
cop - per   bot - tom
fif - ty   mount - ed

tim - pa - ni   in   horse   pla - toons, ____   Thun - der - ing,
can - non   in   the   bat - ter - y, _____   Thun - der - ing,

thun - der - ing, all a - long the way. Dou - ble bell eu -
thun - der - ing, loud - er than be - fore. Clar - i - nets of

1.

pho - ni - ums and big bas - soons, ___ Each bas - soon ___
ev - 'ry size and

2.

___ hav - ing his big fat say. There were trum - pet - ers who'd

16

im - pro - vise a full oc - tave high - er than the score.

(A) *Chorus*

Sev - en - ty six trom - bones hit the coun - ter - point, ___ while a hun - dred and

ten cor - nets blazed a - way. ___ To the rhy - thm of

Harch! Harch! Harch! All the kids be - gan to march, and they're

march - ing still right to - day. ___

MAJOR and MINOR

It's Up to You and Me

Words and Music by Jill Jackson and Sy Miller

REFRAIN

It's up to you and me, my friend, It's up to you and me. If there's
ev-er to be __ an-y peace on earth, It's up to you __ and me. __

VERSE

1. We all saw the plan-et earth, shin-ing there in space,
2. We've been kill-ing ev-'ry-thing, man and na-ture too,
3. Chil-dren learn from what we do, more than what we say,
4. We must learn to love, my friend, earth's our on-ly school.
5. If we want to change the world, it can on-ly be

Look at the **refrain** and **verse** of this song. Which section is in a major tonality and which section is in a minor tonality?

Listen to another song about taking care of our planet. *Pass It On Down* is sung by the popular country group Alabama. You can join in on the refrain.

Pass It On Down ....Teddy Gentry, Randy Owen, Will Robinson, and Ronnie Rogers

Pass It On Down *Refrain*

So, let's leave some blue up above us,
Let's leave some green on the ground.
It's only ours to borrow,
Let's save some for tomorrow,
Leave it and pass it on down.

We know the earth is home, my friend, to all _____ the hu - man race.
We bet - ter stop this trend, or it's the end _____ of me and you.
Wheth-er they live to learn at all is up _____ to us to - day.
We'd bet - ter start this ver - y day to live _____ the gold - en rule.
If you be - gin by chang-ing you and I, _____ by chang-ing me.

Coda

Dm   A₇

peace on earth, It's up to you _____ and

Repeat and fade

Dm   A₇   Dm   A₇   Dm   A₇

me. It's up to you and   me, It's up to you and   me, It's up to you and

Dm   A₇   Dm   A₇

me, It's up to you and   me, It's up to you and

Song of the Canallers

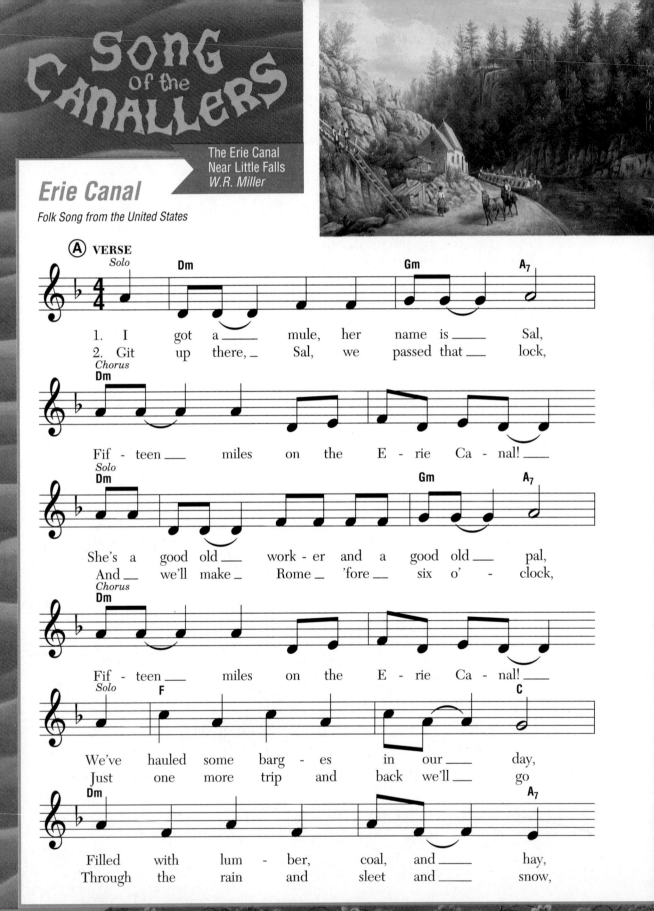

The Erie Canal
Near Little Falls
W.R. Miller

Erie Canal

Folk Song from the United States

(A) VERSE

Solo

Dm · Gm · A₇

1. I got a _____ mule, her name is _____ Sal,
2. Git up there, _ Sal, we passed that _ lock,

Chorus

Dm

Fif - teen _____ miles on the E - rie Ca - nal! _____

Solo

Dm · Gm · A₇

She's a good old _ work - er and a good old _ pal,
And _ we'll make _ Rome _ 'fore _ six o' - clock,

Chorus

Dm

Fif - teen _____ miles on the E - rie Ca - nal! _____

Solo

F · C

We've hauled some barg - es in our _____ day,
Just one more trip and back we'll _ go

Dm · A₇

Filled with lum - ber, coal, and _____ hay,
Through the rain and sleet and _____ snow,

The Erie Canal was opened in 1825. It was a busy waterway between Albany and Buffalo, New York, providing an important link between the Great Lakes and the Atlantic Ocean.

The boats were pulled along by mules or horses that walked on the towpath, at the side of the canal. The words of this song express the affection the canaller had for his mule.

Listen to the recording and discover the tonality of each section.

And we know ev - 'ry inch of the way
'Cause we know ev - 'ry inch of the way
From Al - ba - ny to Buf - fa - lo.

B REFRAIN
Chorus

Low bridge, ev - 'ry - bod - y down,

Low bridge, 'cause we're com - ing to a town;

And you'll al - ways know your neigh-bor, You'll al - ways know your pal,

If you ev - er nav - i - gat - ed on the E - rie Ca - nal.

REGISTER — RANGE

In music the word **register** refers to location.
If a group of tones are all high sounds, they are in a high register.
If a group of tones are all low sounds, they are in a low register.

In this music you will hear sounds that are in high and
low registers.

 "Samuel Goldenberg and Schmuyle" from *Pictures
at an Exhibition* .... Modest Mussorgsky

In a melody, the span from the lowest tone to the highest tone is called
range. The range may be narrow or wide.

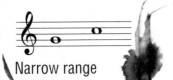

Narrow range   Wide range

The recording of "Haliwa-Saponi Canoe Song" you will hear is a performance by the Haliwa-Saponi Singers. The song does not have words. It uses **vocables**—syllables that do not have particular meaning. Vocables are often a part of Native American music. As you listen, follow the music and find the lowest and highest notes. Is the range of the song narrow or wide?

Haliwa-Saponi Canoe Song

Native American Song of the Haliwa Saponi   *Transcribed by J. Bryan Burton*

Drums
(continue throughout)

We   ya we   we ya   we   we ya we,

Ya we __ ya o - we;   Ya we   ya we we ya we   we ya we,

Fine

Ya we __ ya o - we.   Ya we ha ya we ha   yo - we;

Ya   we __ ya o - we.   Ya we ha ya we ha   yo - we;

1.
Ya   we __ ya o - we.   Ya

2.   *D.S. al Fine*
we __ ya o - we.

© 1992 World Music Press. Used by Permission.

ARABIAN

Once upon a time there was a sultan, or king, named Shahriyar. He thought all women were disloyal. So he decided to marry a new sultana every evening and put her to death the next morning. Of course, there was no happiness in becoming the sultana. But the daughter of a government official, Scheherazade, offered to become the sultana. She knew she was in danger but was confident of a scheme that would save her life. Her plan was to tell fascinating stories to the sultan. Because the sultan was so curious about how the tales would end, he kept putting off her execution. Scheherazade continued her storytelling for one thousand and one nights, the sultan gave up his ruthless plan, and the couple lived happily ever after.

Rimsky-Korsakov loved the tales of the Arabian Nights and selected some of them to become the background of his composition, *Scheherazade.*

You will hear the third section of *Scheherazade,* called "The Young Prince and the Young Princess." As you listen, notice how the composer paints pictures and tells stories through his use of melody and instrumental tone color.

 "The Young Prince and the Young Princess," Movement 3, from *Scheherazade*..............Nikolay Rimsky-Korsakov

These two themes represent the prince and the princess.

Theme 1—Prince

Theme 2—Princess

NIGHTS' MUSIC

Listen again and this time try to answer the following questions.

- What instruments play the theme of the prince?

- Which words best describe the style of this melody?

  gentle   flowing   march like

  heavy   dark   smooth

- What instrument plays the theme of the princess?

- Is the music in a major or minor tonality?

- What other instruments do you hear?

MEET THE COMPOSER

Nikolay Rimsky-Korsakov

(1844–1908)

A small town in Russia, called Tikhvin, was the birthplace of Nikolay Andreyevich Rimsky-Korsakov. His father loved opera. His mother played the piano and often sang Russian folk songs and told Russian folk tales to her young son. When he was twelve years old, he entered the naval college at St. Petersburg. Later, as an officer in the Russian navy, he sailed around the world and visited many countries, including the United States.

Rimsky-Korsakov loved to tell stories through music. Many of the operas, songs, and symphonies he wrote have Russian folk themes. His music is full of exciting color and rich texture.

The Sound of Voices

Your voice has a special sound, called **tone color**, whether you use it to whisper, speak, shout, or sing. Every person in the world has a voice that sounds different from every other voice.

Some people's singing voices are high and some people's singing voices are low. Most *young* children have high singing voices.

Listen to the voices on the recording of "Chester." Who is singing?

Chester

Words and Music by William Billings

1. Let ty - rants shake their i - ron rod
2. What grate - ful of - f'ring shall _____ we bring,

And slav - 'ry clank _____ her gall - ing chains;
What shall we ren - der to _____ the Lord?

We fear them not, We ___ trust _____ in God;
Loud hal - le - lu - jahs ___ let _____ us sing,

New ___ Eng - land's God _____ for - ev - er reigns.
And ___ praise His name _____ on ev - 'ry chord.

A Quartet of Voices

Adult singers are grouped according to the tone color and register (highness or lowness) of their voices.

- Soprano: high woman's voice

- Alto: low woman's voice

- Tenor: high man's voice

- Bass: low man's voice

Listen to another version of "Chester." Do you hear men's voices, or women's voices? How is this version of "Chester" different from the one on page 98?

Chester, Version 2.................William Billings

"Chester" was written by William Billings, one of America's earliest composers. The song was used as a marching song by the Continental Army during the Revolutionary War.

William Schuman, an American who lived in this century, wrote a set of three pieces, a triptych, based on themes by William Billings. The last movement, which recaptures Billings's deep religious and patriotic feelings, uses the melody of "Chester."

As you listen, try to decide whether the theme is always heard as a whole or whether it is broken into pieces.

"Chester" from New England Triptych
.................William Schuman

VOCAL ENSEMBLES

Duet

Music that is written for two performers to sing or play is called a **duet**.

"Four Strong Winds" is arranged for two voices. Listen to the recording. What combination of voices do you hear?

When you know the song, team up with a friend and try singing "Four Strong Winds" as a duet.

Four Strong Winds   from *Song to a Seagull*

Words and Music by Ian Tyson   Arranged by Robert Evans

VERSE

1. Think I'll go   out to Al - ber - ta Wea-ther's good there in the   fall,
2. If I get there be-fore the   snow flies And if things are go-ing good,

Got some friends that I   can   go   to work - in'   for, _____
You could meet me if   I   sent you down the   fare. _____

Still I   wish you'd change your mind If I   asked you one more time,
But by   then it would be   winter, Ain't too   much for you to   do,

But we've been through that a   hun-dred times or   more. _____
And those winds sure   can blow cold a - way out   there. _____

© 1963 (Renewed) Warner Bros. Inc. All rights reserved. Used by permission.

Trio

Music that is written for three performers to sing or play is called a **trio**.

As you listen to the selections listed below, think about the following.

What combination of voices do you hear in each piece?

Are the pieces in the same style, or are they in different styles?

 The Alphabet ....Wolfgang Amadeus Mozart

 Boogie Woogie Bugle Boy ....Prince/Raye

REFRAIN

Four strong winds that blow lone-ly, Sev - en seas that run high,

All those things that don't change come what may, _____

But our good times are all gone, And I'm bound for mov - in' on,

I'll look for you if I'm ev - er back this way. _____

Quartets in Close Harmony

Here is an old song that was popular during the
days of the Civil War. Are the voices on the recording
singing the same part or are they singing in harmony?
Are the voices accompanied by instruments?

Aura Lee

Words by W.W. Fosdick   Music by George R. Poulton

1. As the black-bird in the spring, 'Neath the wil - low tree
2. On her cheek the rose was born, Mu - sic when she spoke.

Sat and piped, I heard him sing, Sing - ing Au - ra Lee.
In her eyes the rays of morn In - to splen-dor broke.

REFRAIN

Au - ra Lee, Au - ra Lee, Maid with gold - en hair!

Sun-shine came a - long with thee, And swal-lows in the air.

Listen to the voices on this recording of *Aura Lee*. What do you hear?

 Aura Lee ....W. W. Fosdick and George Poulton

In this next recording, you will hear another group of voices singing in close harmony. What kinds of voices do you hear?

 Cabaret ....Fred Ebb and George Kander

This version of *Amazing Grace* might be heard in some churches today. How is it different from the first recording you heard?

 Amazing Grace, Version 2
..............Early American Melody

Singing Schools

If you had lived in earlier times, you might have attended a singing school. You might have used music that was written in a strange-looking notation called shape notes. Each note head represented a syllable.

fa   sol   la   mi

Here is what the music of *Amazing Grace* looked like in those singing-school days.

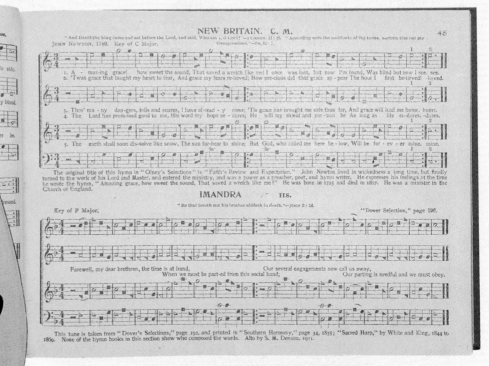

Here is what the music sounded like in those singing-school days.

 Amazing Grace, Version 3
...................Early American Melody

CREATING

Montage—
*Harmony in
Our World*

HARMONY

Look at the refrain of "The World Goes Rolling On."
How is the two-part harmony created?

The World Goes Rolling On

Words and Music by Gershon Kingsley and Robert C. Larimer

1. Ba - bies _ are cry - ing _ and there's no one _ to lis - ten, _
2. Bel - lies _ are growl - ing _ and there's no one _ to feed them, _
3. Man - kind _ is yearn - ing _ for a hu - man _ e - qua - tion, _
4. We have _ a vi - sion _ of a world with - out cha - os, _

And old folks _ are dy - ing _ and there's no one _ to miss them. _
And peo - ple _ are howl - ing _ and there's no one _ to lead them. _
And slow - ly _ we're turn - ing _ to the new gen - er - a - tion. _
A prac - ti - cal vi - sion _ be - cause with or _ with - out us _

REFRAIN

1,2,3. But still the world goes roll - ing on and on,
4. The world will still go roll - ing on and on,

And still the world goes roll - ing on. _____
And we would like to ride a - long. _____

echoing the melody

How is the harmony part created in this song?

Let's Go Singin'

Words and Music by Dianne Baker

A **REFRAIN**

1: Let's go sing - in' ___ down that road. ___

2: Let's go sing - in' ___ down that road ___

1: ___ Let's go sing - in' ___ where ev - er we go. ___

2: ___ Let's go sing - in', ___ sing-in' ev'ry-where we

1: This road is rock-y, ___ life's not eas-y, ___ this ___ we

2: go. This road is rock-y, ___ life's not eas-y, ___ this ___ we

Parts for Percussion

Here are two percussion parts to play with Section A. Can you create other patterns?

Woodblock

Tambourine

Fine

1

know, So we'll go sing-in' ___ where ev-er we go. ___

2

know, So we'll go sing-in' where ev-er we go. ___

B VERSE

1. We'll look to the fu - ture ___ and live each day as it ___ ap-pears,
2. This road's al-ways wind - ing ___ through hills and val-leys of ___ our mind.

Each sun - rise, oh, so pre-cious, with its hopes and fears. _
Dark clouds are drift-in' o - ver, may be sil - ver lined. _

We're in this to-geth - er ___ The time is not so long; ___
We'll not be dis-cour - aged _ We'll see the sun be-fore too long.

D.C.

We'll make the most of what _ we _ have, Sing-in' a song. _
We'll make the most of what _ we _ have, Sing-in' a song. _

TWO-PART HARMONY

Follow the music as you listen to the recording of "The *John B.* Sails."
Compare the contour, or shape, of the bottom line of notes with the melody.

The "John B." Sails

Folk Song from the Bahama Islands

(A) VERSE

1. Oh, we come on ___ the sloop *John* B. My
2. The ___ first mate ___ he got sad,
3. The ___ poor cook ___ he got fits, And

grand - fa - ther and me, A - round Nas - sau ___
Feel - in' ___ aw - fly bad, Captain come a -
throw way ___ all the grits, Then he took and ___

Town we ___ did roam. ___ Walk - in' all
board, took him a - way. ___ Please let me a -
eat up all of the corn. ___ Please let me go

night Just see - in' the sights, Well, I
lone And let ___ me go home, Well, I
home, I want ___ to go home, Well, this

Intervals

In two-part harmony, the distance between the bottom note and top note is called an **interval**.

interval

We can name the interval by calling the bottom note *1* and counting to the top note

feel so break up, — I want to go home.
feel so break up, — I want to go home.
is the worst trip — Since I _____ was born.

B REFRAIN

So hoist up ___ the *John B.* sails,

See how ___ the main - s'l set, Send for ___ the Cap-t'n a -

shore, Let ___ me go home. Please let ___ me go

home, I want ___ to go home. Well, ___ I

feel so break ___ up, — I want ___ to go home.

MORE TWO-PART HARMONY

Section A is in **unison**—everyone sings the same part.
A harmony part is added in Section B.
How does the texture of the music change when the harmony part is added?

Harmony

Words and Music by Norman Simon and Artie Simon

1. The time has come, Let us be - gin, with all our voic - es
2. Like the shep - herd guards his sheep, Watch your chil - dren

join - ing in, ____ To sing of love and broth - er - hood, __
as they sleep, __ And like the pot - ter turns his clay, ____

And peo - ple do - ing what they should to help their fel - low
Oh, help us shape a bet - ter day and let us sing a

man be free, And fill this land with har - mo - ny, ____
song of love, And there's one thing I'm cer - tain of, ____

The young, the old, the rich, the poor, __ Mak - ing sounds
Love will fill the hearts of men, __ And peace will come

nev - er heard be - fore. _____ La la la la la
on _ earth a - gain. _____

B **REFRAIN**

Har - mo - ny, __ har - mo - ny, __ let's all join in

har - mo - ny, __ And sing a - way _ the hurt and fear, _ A

1.

2.

great new day will soon _ be _ here. ___

here. ___

THREE-PART HARMONY

The harmony in "Kum Ba Yah" is based on the F, B♭ and C₇ chords.
Each of the chords is built on a tone of the F-major scale. The tone on which the **chord** is built is called the **root**.

Kum Ba Yah

Traditional Song from Africa

Kum ba yah, my Lord, Kum ba yah! Kum ba yah, my Lord, Kum ba yah! Kum ba yah, my Lord, Kum ba yah! Oh, Lord, _____ Kum ba yah!

Join with two of your classmates and play a chordal accompaniment for "Kum Ba Yah." Follow the chord names on the music.

LAYERS OF SOUND

The words of this folk song from Liberia mean, "Don't cry, pretty little girl, don't cry."

How many different sections are in this song? Can you find the signs that tell you to sing each section two times?

On the recording, you will hear how the sections (layers of sound) are put together.

Banuwa

Folk Song from Liberia

(1) Ba - nu - wa, ba - nu - wa, ba - nu - wa yo. ____

(2) Ba - nu - wa, ba - nu - wa, ba - nu - wa yo. ____ (3)

(3) A - la - no, neh - ni a - la - no;

a - la - no, neh - ni a - la - no.

Listen to some dance music played by drummers of the Nyamwezi tribe in East Africa, and then **improvise** your own drum part as the class sings "Banuwa."

Manyanga Drum Rhythms
............Nyamwezi Drummers

④

Neh - ni a - la - no;   Neh - ni a - la - no.

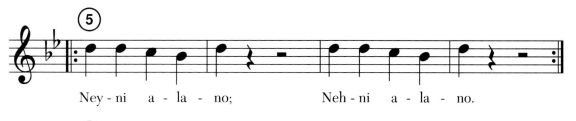

⑤

Ney - ni a - la - no;   Neh - ni a - la - no.

⑥

Ba - nu - wa,   ba - nu - wa,   ba - nu - wa yo. ____

CALL AND RESPONSE

Like many African songs, this song from Uganda is in call-and-response style. Can you describe the difference in texture between the calls and the responses?

The Peacock   *English Words by Beatrice Landeck*   *Folk Song from Uganda*   *Collected by the Grail Singers*

Call

Oh, where goes he? _____

Response

He goes out to find a bird, the pea-cock. _

Ma - na - ku - ba! _____

Ma - ma knows that he will find the pea-cock. _

From record "Grail Singers Folk Songs," The Grail, Loveland, Ohio

Once you have learned the song, try adding one or more of these percussion parts.

Ta - ta - na - ku - ba! _____

Ta knows that   he will find the   pea - cock. _

Oh, Ba - ba - na - ku - ba! _____

Ba knows that   he will find the   pea - cock. _

TWO CHORAL COMPOSITIONS

Judith Lang Zaimont, born in 1945, is a living, well-known American composer.

Johannes Brahms, who lived from 1833 to 1897, was a German composer.

These composers are from different worlds and different times. Their music has a very different sound.

You will hear the following choral compositions—pieces that are sung.

 Serenade: To Music (excerpt)
...............Judith Lang Zaimont

 Liebeslieder Waltzes, Op. 65, No. 8
.................Johannes Brahms

A CENTURY APART

Make two columns on a piece of paper and label one *same* and the other *different*. As you listen, think about what is the same and what is different about the two pieces. You may choose descriptions from the list below to put into your two categories, or you may write your own descriptions.

Sung by adult men and women

Starts softly and gets gradually louder

English words

No accompaniment

Piano accompaniment

Thin texture

Thick texture

Everyone singing all the time

Has a distinct melody

A meter you can conduct

Clashing sounds

Voices entering at different times

Big variation in dynamics from soft to loud

Chamber Ensembles

There was a time when there were few public concerts to attend, no radios or stereos to listen to, and no television to watch. In those days, if people wanted to enjoy music, they had to make their own.

It was not uncommon for small groups of friends to gather at a home and make music for their own pleasure. The music that these small groups of instrumentalists played became known as **chamber music** because it was performed in a chamber, or room, rather than in a large concert hall.

Some of the world's greatest music was written for chamber ensembles, and chamber music is still being composed today.

Each selection listed below is performed by a small instrumental **ensemble**. As you listen to each piece, try to answer these questions.

- How many players are performing?

- Do all the instruments seem to be from one family?

- What individual instruments do you hear?

 String Quartet No. 1 in E-Flat (Op. 12), Movement 2, "Canzonetta" ....Felix Mendelssohn

 Fugue in G Minor ("Little") ....Johann Sebastian Bach

Trois pièces brèves ("Three Short Pieces") *for Wind Quintet, No. 1*...........Jacques Ibert

Piece for CHAMBER ORCHESTRA

Johann Sebastian Bach is considered to be one of the greatest composers who ever lived. You are going to hear the last **movement** of a piece he wrote for four solo instruments accompanied by strings and harpsichord. It is called the *Brandenburg Concerto*, *No. 2*.

As you listen, try to answer the following questions.

• Is the beat strong and steady?

• Is the tempo fast or slow?

• Is the music lively or serene?

• Can you identify any of the solo instruments?

Brandenburg Concerto, No. 2, Movement 3
.................Johann Sebastian Bach

This rhythm pattern is used repeatedly. Try clapping it or tapping it on your desk.

Listen for this theme. Can you hear it as it is played by each solo instrument? When is it played by the low strings in the accompaniment part?

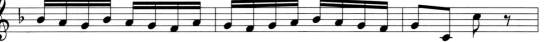

MEET THE COMPOSER

Johann Sebastian Bach

(1685–1750)

When Johann Sebastian Bach was born, the Bach family had been musicians for a number of years. All the members of this large German family could sing or play the harpsichord, organ, or violin. Johann Sebastian was no exception. As soon as his hands were big enough to hold a violin, his father began to teach him to play. But it was the organ that became Johann Sebastian's favorite instrument.

For many years, Bach was the choir director and organist of Saint Thomas's Church in the city of Leipzig. This German city was the center for great fairs that brought crowds of people to the city every year. As a result, the fame of Bach as an organist and a composer spread all through Germany. Today he is hailed throughout the world as one of the greatest composers of all time.

A Symphony by Beethoven

The conductor's **score** below shows the first eight measures of Beethoven's *Symphony No. 1*, Movement 3.

🎧 *Symphony No. 1*, Movement 3 ....Ludwig van Beethoven

MEET THE COMPOSER

Ludwig van Beethoven

(1770–1827)

Ludwig van Beethoven was born into a poor but musical family. His father was his first teacher. The young Beethoven began to study piano when he was four years old. He played in public when he was eight, and by the time he was eleven, he had written and published three piano sonatas. A few years later, Beethoven went to Vienna. The music lovers of that Austrian city soon recognized Beethoven's amazing ability as a pianist and later appreciated his genius as a composer.

No one knows exactly when Beethoven wrote his *Symphony No. 1*. We do know, however, that its first performance was in Vienna on April 2, 1800. We also know that Beethoven himself conducted the performance.

What does the score tell you about the tempo? The **dynamics**? Which instruments will play?

Here are the themes that Beethoven used in *Symphony No. 1*, Movement 3. You might want to play each theme on a keyboard before you listen to the recording.

A Symphony by Beethoven

The themes are color coded to help you hear what is going on in the music.

Symphony No. 1, Movement 3 ....Ludwig van Beethoven

CALL CHART 4

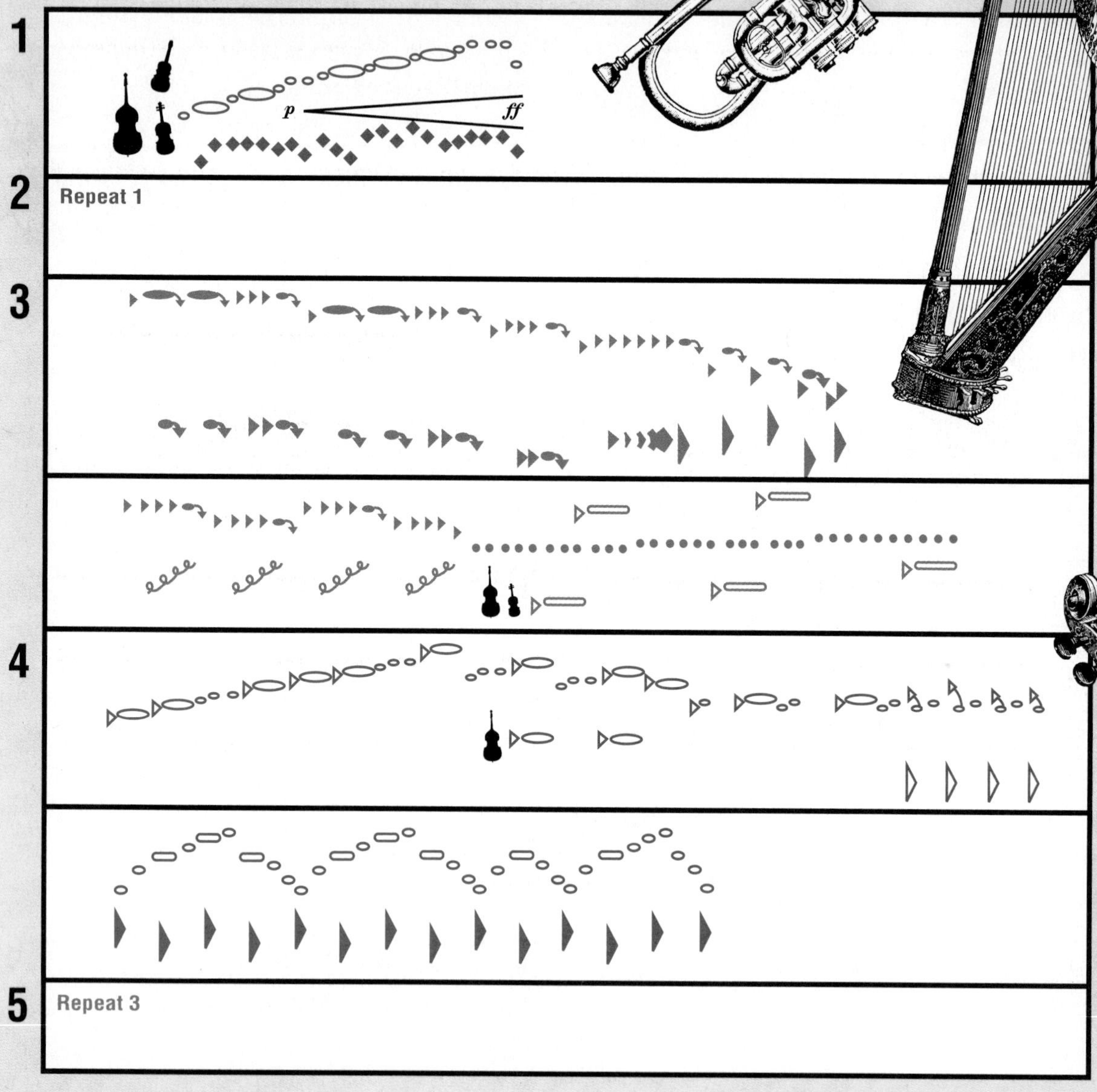

1 p ff

2 Repeat 1

3

4

5 Repeat 3

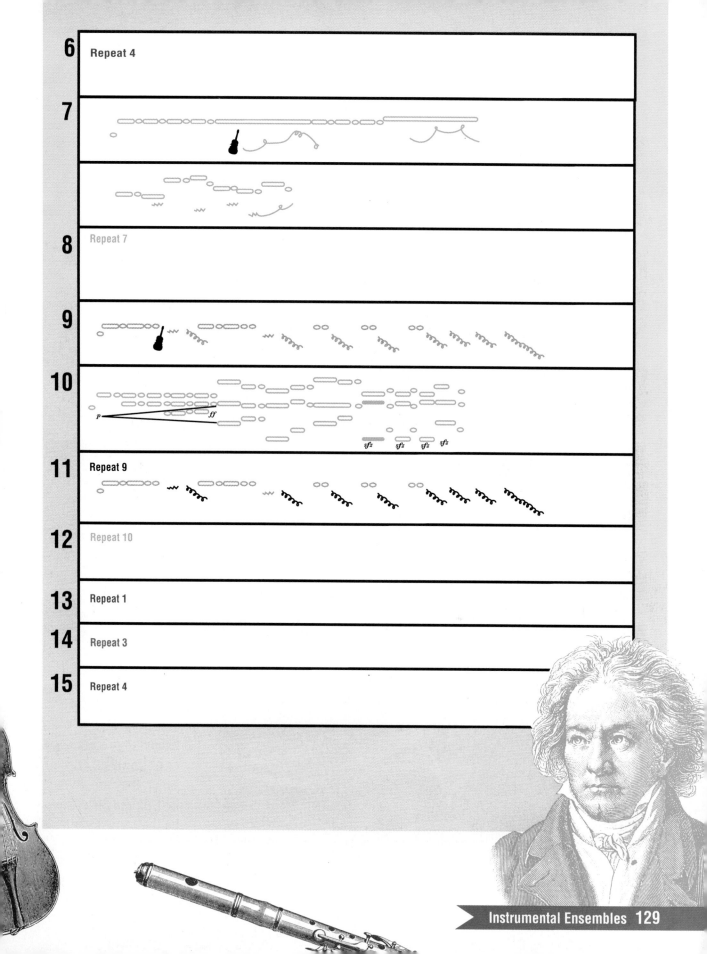

PERCUSSION ENSEMBLES

Percussion instruments are probably as old as civilization itself. Any instrument that you hit, rub, or shake is a percussion instrument. When you pat your knees or clap your hands, your body is a percussion instrument.

Some percussion instruments, like the xylophone, play definite pitches. Others, like the maracas, produce a particular color of sound with no definite pitch.

Listen carefully to the following recordings of percussion ensembles from different parts of the world. Can you think of some similarities and differences among the ensembles?

Often, **percussion** instruments are played in groups or ensembles. When they are, the instruments may all be the same except for their size.

Marimba Ensemble of Zimbabwe

The Young Person's Guide to the Orchestra,
Op. 34, (excerpt) ....Benjamin Britten

The percussion section of the Western symphony orchestra is made up of a variety of percussion instruments. In this recording, the percussion section is featured as a soloist.

Drum Corps from England

Percussion instruments are played in every country of the world. Frequently they are associated with ceremonies. In this group, all the drummers play the same rhythms at the same time on identical instruments.

Dou Dou Rose Ensemble from Senegal

Drums are particularly important in the music of Africa.

PENSEZ c. ... ŒUVRES

Gamelan is a kind of orchestra found mainly in Indonesia and Malaysia. These orchestras can include metallophones, xylophones, gongs, gong-chimes, drums, wind and string instruments.

Gamelan of Indonesia

Many percussion instruments have an ancient history. But the steel drums from Trinidad were invented in the 1940s. They are made out of large oil cans.

Mary Ann.......Steel Band

THEMES

Let's explore music through
the THEME connection.

You will find music of different
styles, music for movement, music from
films and Broadway shows, opera and oratorio,
music from the many places Americans
come from, music of our past and present,
patriotic music, and music to
celebrate special holidays.

You will also learn a musical
based on the writing of our Constitution—
a special theme to connect
music and social studies.

section 2

How do you think the composer of this song feels about singing? Read the words to find out. How does singing make *you* feel?

Clap the steady beat as you sing with the recording.

I Shall Sing

Words and Music by Van Morrison

1. I shall sing, — sing my song, — be it right, — be it wrong. —
   heart, — with my soul, — for the young, - for the old. ____

— In the night, — in the day, — an - y - how, — an - y - way. —
— When I'm hap - py, when I'm low, — when I'm fast — when I'm slow. —

— I shall sing:
— I shall sing: La la la la la la la la, La la la la la la la la,

Singing is often a part of special occasions. Can you think of different kinds of celebrations when people sing?

Tap or walk the steady beat as you listen to this popular song.

Celebration (excerpt) ....Kool & the Gang

la la la la la la la___ la la la___ la,   La la la la la la la,

La la la la la la la la,   la la la la la la la___ la la la___ la.

3   1. C₇   2.   F   *Repeat and fade*

2. With my   La la la la la la la la,

La la la la la la la la,   la la la la la la la___ la la la___ la.

This song was sung at the 1988 summer Olympic games that were held in Seoul, South Korea. Why is "One Moment in Time" an appropriate song for the Olympics?

One Moment in Time

Words and Music by Albert Hammond and John Bettis

Each day I live, I want to be a day to give the best of me. I'm on-ly one, but not a-lone. My fin-est day is yet un-known. I broke my heart for ev-'ry gain. / be the ver-y best. To taste the sweet, I want it all, I faced the / no time for pain. I rise and fall, yet through it all this much re-mains: / less. I've laid the plans, now lay the chance here in my hands: I want one mo-ment in time when I'm more than I thought I could be, when all of my dreams are a heart-beat a-way and the an-swers are all up to me. Give me one mo-ment in time when I'm rac-ing with des-ti-ny.

WINNER

Then, in that one mo-ment in time, I will feel, I will feel eter-ni-

ty. I've lived to feel e-ter-ni-ty. You're a win-ner

for a life-time. If you seize that one mo-ment in time, make it

B

shine. Give me one mo-ment in time, when I'm more than I thought I could

be, when all of my dreams are a heart-beat a-way and the

an-swers are all up to me. Give me one mo-ment in

time, when I'm rac-ing with des-ti-ny. Then, in that one

mo-ment in time I will be, I will be, I will be free.

Name the States

Fifty Nifty United States

Words and Music by Ray Charles

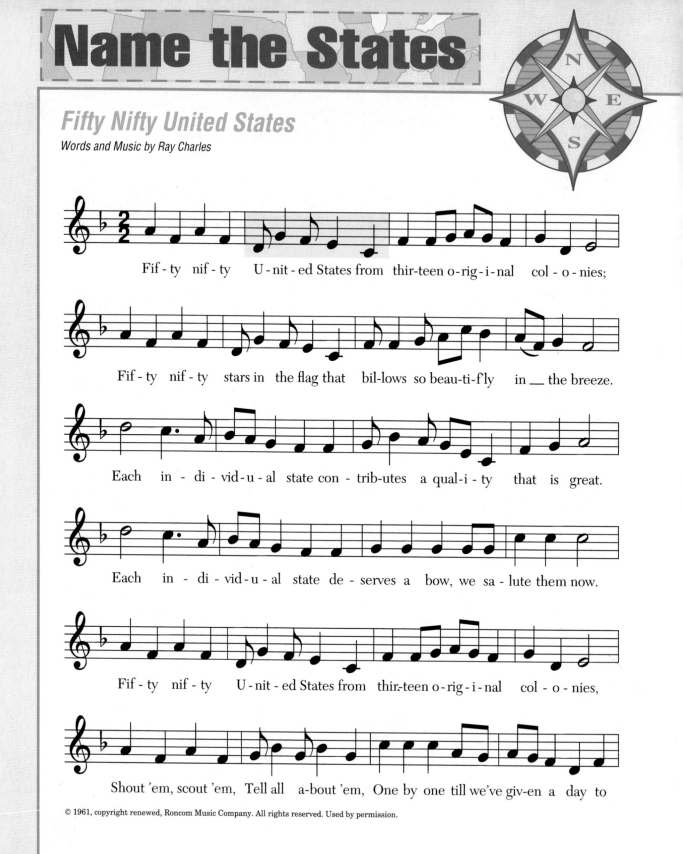

Fif-ty nif-ty U-nit-ed States from thir-teen o-rig-i-nal col-o-nies;

Fif-ty nif-ty stars in the flag that bil-lows so beau-ti-f'ly in __ the breeze.

Each in-di-vid-u-al state con-trib-utes a qual-i-ty that is great.

Each in-di-vid-u-al state de-serves a bow, we sa-lute them now.

Fif-ty nif-ty U-nit-ed States from thir-teen o-rig-i-nal col-o-nies,

Shout 'em, scout 'em, Tell all a-bout 'em, One by one till we've giv-en a day to

Sing out the name of your own state when you
come to the color box on page 145. Add
movement for a special performance of this song.

ev - 'ry state   in the U. S. A.   Al - a -

bam - a,   A - las - ka, Ar - i - zo - na, Ar - kan - sas,   Cal - i -

for - nia, Col - o - ra - do,   Con - nect - i - cut;

Del - a - ware,   Flor - i - da,   Geor - gia,   Ha - wai - i,   I - da -

ho,   Il - li - nois,   In - di - an - a;

I - o - wa,   Kan - sas, Ken - tuck - y, Lou - i - si - an - a, Maine,

Mar - y - land,   Mas - sa - chu - setts, Mich - i - gan;   Min - ne -

Map 1961   *Jasper Johns*

North, south, east, west, in our calm ob-jec-tive o-pin-ion, *(name of*

home state) is the best of the Fif-ty nif-ty U-nit-ed States from

thir-teen o-rig-i-nal col-o-nies, Shout 'em, scout 'em, Tell all a-bout 'em,

One by one till we've giv-en a day to ev-'ry state in the good old

U. _____ S. _____ A. _____

Sing Out LOUD

The composer of this song, Joe Raposo, was one of the creators of Sesame Street and its first musical director. He originally wrote the song in Spanish, calling it "Canta." Under its English title, "Sing" was recorded by Bing Crosby, Barbra Streisand, The Carpenters, and other stars.

Sing

Words and Music by Joe Raposo

(sing echo 2nd time)

Sing! Sing! Sing a song. Sing a song. Sing out loud. Sing out loud. Sing out strong. Sing out strong. Sing of good things, not bad. Sing of hap-py, not sad.

Sing! Sing! Sing a song. Sing a song. Make it

Add a Part

The following parts for keyboard or mallet instruments
can be added to the coda.

Player 1

Player 2

Player 3

sim - ple   to   last your whole life   long. _____   Don't

wor-ry that   it's   not   good   e - nough, _ for   an - y - one else   to   hear.

Sing!   Sing   a   song! _____

Coda   *(Repeat and fade)*

La   la la la la, La   la   la la la la, La   la   la la la la la. ___

Follow the Score

Sunny Day

Words and Music by Terre McPheeters

1. Ev-'ry time it rains, I won-der why ____ it makes me sad, ____ it makes me cry, ____ But ev-'ry time I see the sun up a-bove ____ it feels like ev-'ry one's in love. ____

2. I don't want the rain to bring me down, ____ I'd rath-er smile ____ than wear a frown, _ So come _ on _ sun, _ I'm countin' on you ____ to change _ the _ skies to blue. ____

REFRAIN

Send me a sun-ny day, ____ Send me a clear blue sky, ____

Follow the score of "Sunny Day" and watch for *mf* and other signs that suggest how loud or how soft to sing. Do you think these dynamic markings are appropriate for the words of this song?

Sing and Dance

As you listen to "Evening of Roses," look for the special signs that tell you to repeat one of the sections.

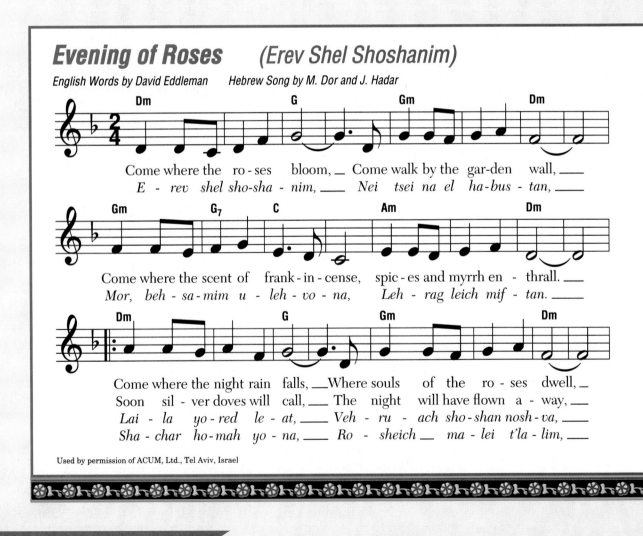

Evening of Roses (Erev Shel Shoshanim)

English Words by David Eddleman   *Hebrew Song by M. Dor and J. Hadar*

Come where the ro-ses bloom, __ Come walk by the gar-den wall, __
E - rev shel sho-sha - nim, ___ Nei tsei na el ha-bus - tan, ___

Come where the scent of frank-in-cense, spic-es and myrrh en - thrall. __
Mor, beh-sa-mim u - leh-vo - na, Leh - rag leich mif - tan.

Come where the night rain falls, __Where souls of the ro-ses dwell, __
Soon sil - ver doves will call, __ The night will have flown a - way, __
Lai - la yo - red le - at, ___ Veh - ru - ach sho-shan nosh-va, __
Sha - char ho-mah yo - na, ___ Ro - sheich __ ma - lei t'la - lim, __

Used by permission of ACUM, Ltd., Tel Aviv, Israel

Joy - ful with love I sing to you, Weav-ing a ten-der _ spell. __
Then will the ro - ses lift their heads Tell - ing the birth of __ day. ___
Ha - va el-chash lach shir ba - lat Ze - mer shel a - ha - va. _____
Pich el ha - bo - ker sho-sha - na, Ek - te fe - nu _ li. _____

Coda

Tell-ing the birth of __ day, _____ Tell-ing the birth of __ day. _____
Ek - te fe - nu _ li, _____ Ek - te fe - nu _ li. _____

SPIRITUAL IN GOSPEL STYLE

As you listen to "Down by the Riverside," keep time to the music with this tap-snap pattern.

(tap snap tap snap)

Down by the Riverside

African American Spiritual

A VERSE

1. Gon - na lay down my sword and shield, __
2. Gon - na join hands with ev - 'ry one, __
3. Gon - na ring out a song of joy, __

Down by the riv - er - side, __

Down by the riv - er - side, __

Down by the riv - er - side, __

Gon - na lay down my sword and shield, __
Gon - na join hands with ev - 'ry one, __
Gon - na ring out a song of joy, __

Accompaniment Patterns

Use these patterns to accompany the singing.

Tambourine

Autoharp
strum

Notice the syncopated patterns as you listen to this spiritual.

This Little Light of Mine
.................African American Spiritual

Down by the riv - er - side, ____

And stud - y _____ war no more. ____

B **REFRAIN**

I ain't gon - na stud - y ____ war no more,

I ain't gon - na stud - y ____ war no more,

I ain't gon - na stud - y _____ war no

1.
more. _____ I ain't gon - na

2.
more. _____

CALL-AND-RESPONSE STYLE

Call-and-response is heard in many songs of western Africa and in many spirituals. Listen for it in "Certainly, Lord."

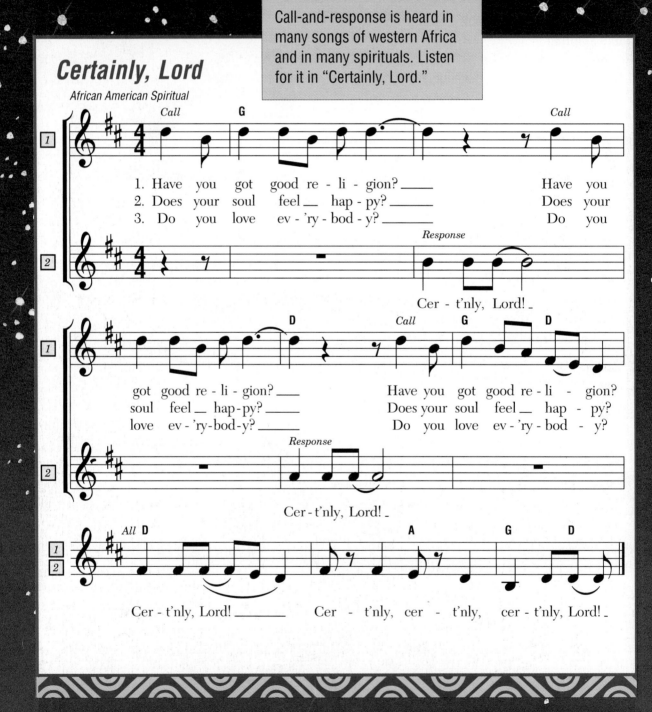

Certainly, Lord

African American Spiritual

1. Have you got good re-li-gion? _____ Have you
2. Does your soul feel _ hap-py? _____ Does your
3. Do you love ev-'ry-bod-y? _____ Do you

Cer-t'nly, Lord!

got good re-li-gion? _____ Have you got good re-li-gion?
soul feel _ hap-py? _____ Does your soul feel _ hap-py?
love ev-'ry-bod-y? _____ Do you love ev-'ry-bod-y?

Cer-t'nly, Lord!

Cer-t'nly, Lord! _____ Cer-t'nly, cer-t'nly, cer-t'nly, Lord!

Add Rhythm Patterns

Try clapping or playing these rhythm patterns as you sing "Certainly, Lord."

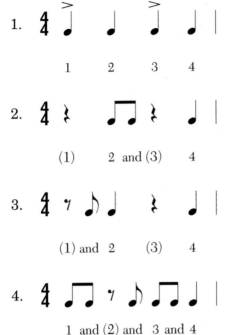

Traveling Shoes is sung by the African American women's vocal group Sweet Honey in the Rock.

Listen for their vocal tone color and the call-and-response style.

Traveling Shoes .... African American Spiritual

A FAMOUS PERFORMING

On this recording, Dr. Walter J. Turnbull, director of The Boys Choir of Harlem, talks about the choir, the choir school, and his role as director.

 Careers in Music—Dr. Walter J. Turnbull

The Boys Choir of Harlem performs music of many periods and styles. Listen as they sing a piece from the 1730s and a traditional African American spiritual.

 "Heavenly Harmony" from Ode for St. Cecilia's Day..................George Frideric Handel

 Nobody Knows the Trouble I've Seen ....African American Spiritual

GROUP

Song FROM A Film

Somewhere Out There *from An American Tail*

Words and Music by James Horner, Barry Mann, and Cynthia Weil

Some-where _ out there be-neath the pale moon - light, _

some - one's think-in' of me and lov - ing me to - night. _

Some-where out _ there _ some-one's say-ing a prayer _____

that we'll find one an - oth-er _____ in that big some - where _ out _

there. And e-ven though I know how ver-y far a-part _ we are, _____

it helps to think _ we might _ be wish - in' on the same _ bright _ star. And

A lost character looking for family and loved ones is a theme of stories told throughout the world. Listen to how the composers use expressive words and melody to describe this longing.

when the night wind starts to sing a lone-some lul-la-by, it

helps to think we're sleep-ing un-der - neath the same big sky.

Some-where out there if love can see us through,

then we'll be to-geth - er some-where out there, out

where dreams come true. _____

An Academy Award Winner

Can you identify all the underwater creatures mentioned in this award-winning song from Disney's *The Little Mermaid*? What musical instruments are mentioned?

Under the Sea
from Disney's *The Little Mermaid*

Words by Howard Ashman   Music by Alan Menken

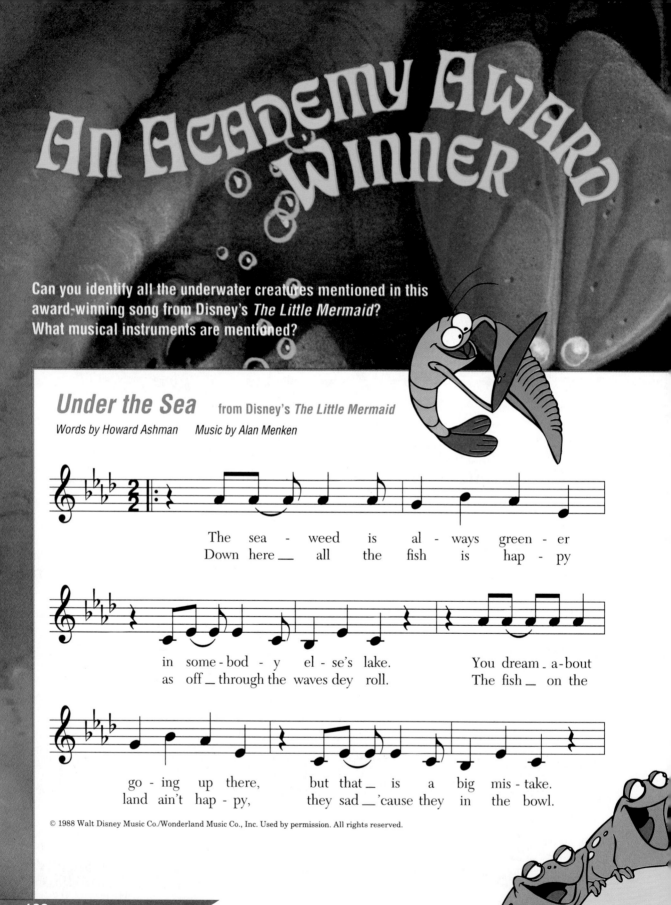

The sea - weed is al - ways green - er
Down here __ all the fish is hap - py

in some - bod - y el - se's lake.   You dream _ a-bout
as off __ through the waves dey roll.   The fish __ on the

go - ing up there,   but that _ is a big mis - take.
land ain't hap - py,   they sad __ 'cause they in the bowl.

Just look＿ at the world a-round you, right here＿ on the
But fish＿ in the bowl is luck-y, they in ＿ for a

o-cean floor.
wors-er fate.

Such won-der-ful things sur-round you,
One day ＿ when the boss get hun-gry

what more＿ is you look-in' for? }
guess who＿ gon' be on the plate. }

Un-der the

sea,

un-der the sea.

Dar - lin' it's bet-ter down _ where it's wet-ter. Take _ it from
No - bod-y beat us, fry _ us and eat us in _ fri-ca -

me. Up _ on the shore they work _ all day. _
see. We _ what the land folks loves _ to cook. _

_ Out _ in the sun they slave _ a - way, ___ while _ we de -
_ Un - der the sea we off _ the hook. _ We _ got no

1.

vo - tin' full _ time to float - in' un - der the sea.
trou-bles, life _ is the bub-bles un - der the

2.

sea.

Un - der the

sea! Since _ life is sweet here we _ got the

beat here nat - u - ral - ly. e - ven the

stur-geon and _ the ray _____ they _ got the urge 'n start _ to play. _

_ We _ got the spir-it, you _ got to hear it un - der the

sea. The newt _ play the flute. The carp _

_ play the harp. The plaice play the bass. And they _sound-in' sharp. The bass _

_ play the brass. The chub _ play the tub. The fluke _

_ is the duke of soul.   The ray _ he can play. The lings _

_ on the strings. The trout _ rock-in' out. The black-fish she sings, The smelt _

_ and the sprat they know _ where it's at,   an' oh, that blow-fish

blow.   Un-der the sea.   Un - der the sea.

When _ the sar - dine be - gin _ the be - guine it's   mu - sic to

me.   What _ do they   got,   a lot _ of sand.

We _ got a hot crus-ta - ce-an band. Each _ lit-tle

clam here know _ how to jam here un - der the sea.

Each _ lit-tle slug here cut - tin' a rug here un - der the

sea. Each _ lit - tle snail here know _ how to

wail here that's _ why its' hot-ter un - der the wa-ter. Ya _ we in

luck here down _ in the muck here un - der the sea. _____

Freedom   from *Shenandoah*

Words by Peter Udell   Music by Gary Geld

1. Free-dom ain't a state like Maine or Vir-gin - ia,
2. Free-dom ain't a boat that's leav-in' with-out ya,
3. Free-dom is a no - tion sweep-in' the na - tion,

Free - dom ain't a - cross some coun - ty line.
Free - dom ain't a place ya float to find.
Free - dom is the right of all man - kind.

Free - dom is a flame that burns with - in ya,
Free - dom is the how ya think a - bout ya, -
Free - dom is a bod - y's 'mag - i - na - tion,

Free-dom's in the state of mind.

B *Chorus*

Free - dom, free - dom, Free - dom, free - dom.

1.,2.

Free - dom is a flame that burns with - in ya,
Free - dom is the how ya think a - bout ya,

Free-dom's in the state ___ of mind.

2

3.

Free - dom is a no - tion sweep - in' the na - tion,

Free - dom is a bod - y's 'mag - i - na - tion,

Free - dom is a full time oc - cu - pa - tion,

Free-dom's in the state ___ of mind!

a *Musical* based on a *Classic Book*

Careers in Music—Daisy Eagan

The Girl I Mean to Be
from *The Secret Garden*

Words by Marsha Norman   *Music by Lucy Simon*

I need a place where I can go Where I can whis-per

what I know Where I can whis-per who I like and where I go to

see them. I need a place where I can hide Where no one sees my

life in-side Where I can make my plans and write them down _ so I can

read them. A place where I can bid my heart be still, and it will

mind _ me A place where I can go when I am lost, and

there I'll find me. I need a place to

spend the day Where no one says to go or stay Where I can take my

pen and draw the girl I mean to be.

"The Magic Flute" A Famous Opera

A comical bird catcher, who has a magic panpipe, claims to have slain a serpent and saved a prince. The three ladies who really killed the snake appear and scold him for lying. They put a padlock on his mouth so he can't tell any more lies. Unbelievable? Not in an **opera** plot.

This part of the story comes in Act I of Mozart's last opera, *The Magic Flute*. The bird catcher's name is Papageno. In the song that introduces him in the opera, he confesses that he catches birds but would much prefer to catch a pretty girl to be his sweetheart.

Listen to the **overture** and then to Papageno's song. The overture is the first music the audience hears when they go to see different types of musical plays. It sets the mood for the performance.

 "Overture" from *The Magic Flute (excerpt)* ....Wolfgang Amadeus Mozart

 "Der Vogelfänger" ("The Bird Catcher") from *The Magic Flute* ....Wolfgang Amadeus Mozart

HANDEL'S BEST KNOWN WORK

There is one piece of music that is often heard during the month of December, when it is performed in thousands of schools, churches, and concert halls, and on radio and TV. It is *Messiah,* an **oratorio** by George Frideric Handel. *Messiah* was first performed in Dublin, Ireland, in 1742, and it is the composer's most famous work.

1 | **Introduction: Strings**

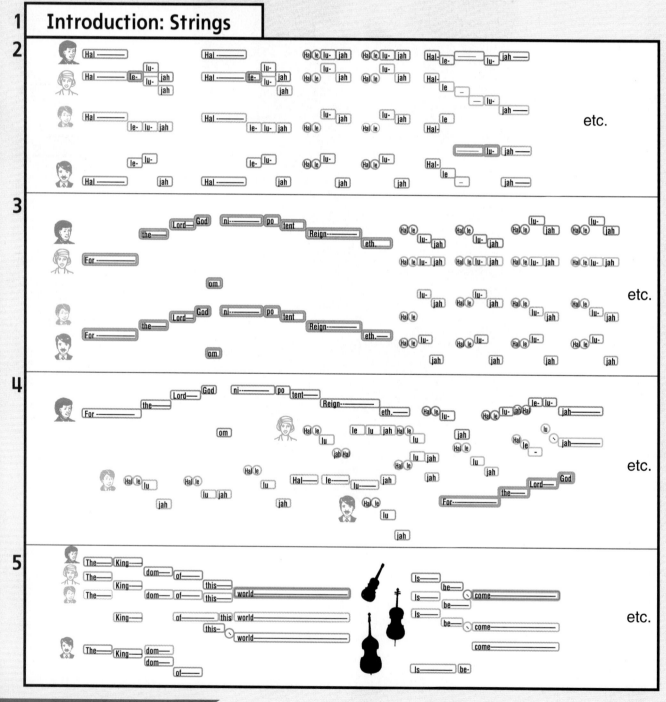

As you follow the chart, listen for the way *Hallelujah* is tossed back and forth from voice to voice. Notice also that one voice sings *For the Lord God omnipotent reigneth* while the other voice sings *Hallelujah!*

"Hallelujah Chorus" from *Messiah*
.................George Frideric Handel

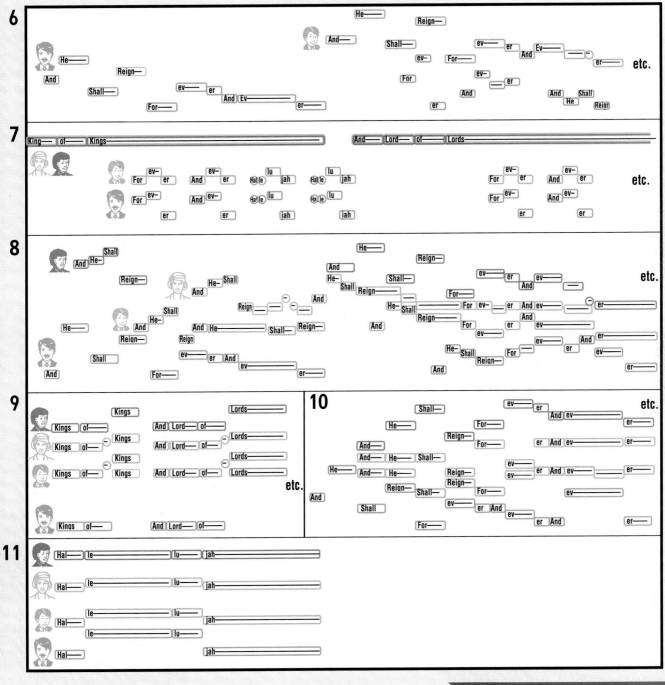

Two-Time Grammy Award Winner Diane Schuur

Diane Schuur, a singer with a rich, joyous sound, won back-to-back Grammy Awards in 1986 and 1987 as "best female jazz singer." On these recordings, Diane Schuur talks about her early life and her career today, and lets us hear her wonderful singing voice.

 Careers in Music—Diane Schuur

 How High the Moon................Hamilton/Lewis

Pollerita

English Words by Aura Kontra   Folk Song from Bolivia

Po - lle - ri - ta, po - lle - ri - ta   that's what   she's wear - ing,
Po - lle - ri - ta, po - lle - ri - ta   de   mi   cho - li - ta,

Po - lle - ri - ta, po - lle - ri - ta   with none   com - par - ing.
Po - lle - ri - ta, po - lle - ri - ta   co - lor   ro - si - ta.

You're made   for   danc - ing,   you're made   for   sing - ing
Que   bien   se   bai - la,   que   bien   se   can - ta,

1.
to   my *cha - ran - gui - to.*
con   mi cha - ran - gui - to.

2.
to   my *cha - ran - gui - to.*
con   mi   cha - ran - gui - to.

Grind - ing   corn   is   not   for   you,   nei - ther   cook   nor   boil   a   stew,
Sa - ra   ma - la - gu   ta   tu   ma - na   tri - go   pe - la - cu

Sing   and   dance   the   whole   day   through.
Ma - na   chu - no   pun - ti - co.

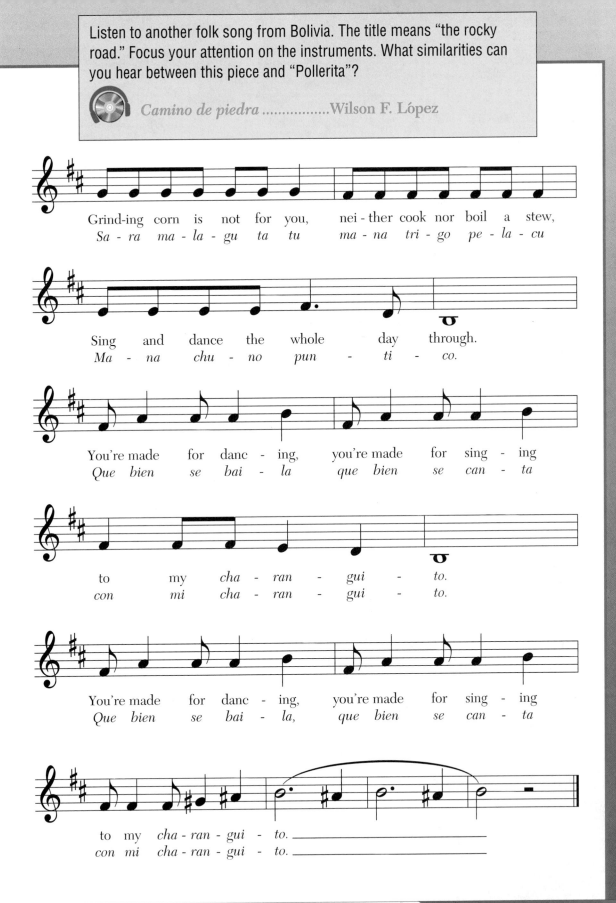

Camino de piedra ....Wilson F. López

Grind-ing corn is not for you, nei-ther cook nor boil a stew,
Sa - ra ma - la - gu ta tu ma - na tri - go pe - la - cu

Sing and dance the whole day through.
Ma - na chu - no pun - ti - co.

You're made for danc - ing, you're made for sing - ing
Que bien se bai - la que bien se can - ta

to my cha - ran - gui - to.
con mi cha - ran - gui - to.

You're made for danc - ing, you're made for sing - ing
Que bien se bai - la, que bien se can - ta

to my cha - ran - gui - to. _____
con mi cha - ran - gui - to. _____

SOUTH OF THE BORDER

When you listen to the recording of this song, you will hear the voices singing in two parts. How are the parts alike? How are they different? Following the score will help you answer the questions.

Laredo

English Words by Margaret Marks   *Folk Song from Mexico*

1. I'm off for __ La - re - do, fare - well, __ my love, I'm
   Ya me voy __ pa - ra el La - re - do __ mi bien, Te
2. I've brought you __ a hand - sewn sad - dle, __ my love, A
   Toma e - sa __ lla - vi - ta de o - ro, __ mi bien, Abre

sor - ry __ to cause you pain; I prom - ise __ to send a
ven - go a __ de - cir a - diós. Ya me voy __ pa - ra el La -
blan - ket __ and bri - dle fine; So when you __ go past the
mi pe - cho y ve - rás; Toma e - sa __ lla - vi - ta

let - ter __ my love, To say when _ we'll meet a - gain.
re - do, __ mi bien, Te ven - go a __ de - cir a - diós.
bunk - house, __ my love, The cow - boys _ will know you're mine.
de o - ro, __ mi bien, Abre mi pe - cho y ve - rás:

Don't fol - low __ a - cross the prai - rie, __ my love, Don't
De a - llá __ te man - do de - cir, __ mi bien, Co -
I've brought you __ a key of sil - ver, __ my love, At -
Lo mu - cho __ que yo te quie - ro, __ mi bien, y el

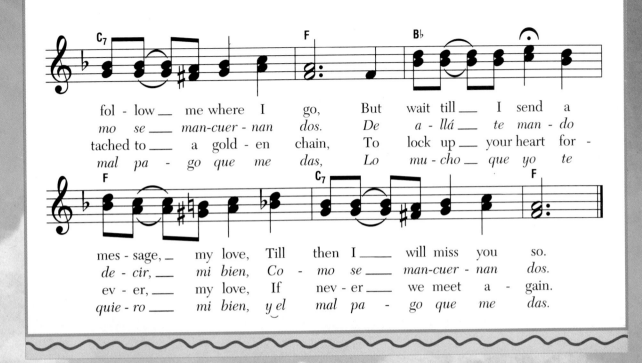

fol - low __ me where	I	go,	But	wait till __	I send	a
mo se __ man-cuer - nan		dos.	De	a - llá __	te man - do
tached to __ a gold - en		chain,	To	lock up __	your heart	for -
mal pa - go que me		das,	Lo	mu - cho __	que yo	te

mes - sage, __	my love,	Till	then I __	will miss	you	so.
de - cir, __	mi bien,	Co -	mo se __	man-cuer - nan		dos.
ev - er, __	my love,	If	nev - er __	we meet	a -	gain.
quie - ro __	mi bien,	y el	mal pa -	go que	me	das.

The American composer Aaron Copland tried to capture the feeling of Mexican music in his piece *El salón México*. Listen to the music and try to identify parts of melodies from two songs in your book—"Laredo" and "Jesusita."

El salón México (excerpt)
..............Aaron Copland

Folk Song from Puerto Rico

This Puerto Rican song tells about a bird who is sad and lonely. As he wanders from place to place, the bird sings so no one will know how unhappy he is.

What is the bird searching for?

The Wandering Bird   *(El pájaro errante)*

Folk Song from Puerto Rico

I am a lone-ly wan-der-er, Al-ways lost, I go
Soy pa-ja-ri-llo er-ran-te que an-da per-di-do, que an-

soar-ing all a-lone. I fly to tall cool trees, tall and
da per-di-do, y va por la en-ra-ma-da en

leaf-y trees, Search-ing for a home. _____
pos de a-bri-go, en pos de a-bri-go. _____

from A BOOK OF BALLADS, SONGS AND SNATCHES, by Haig and Regina Shekerjian, Copyright © 1966 by Haig and Regina Shekerjian. Reprinted by permission of Harper & Row, Publishers, Inc.

Three Ostinatos for Percussion

You can use one of these ostinatos to accompany "The Wandering Bird." Which pattern will you choose? Play it all through the song.

Music has always been an important part of African life. It can be heard in the cities, on the farms, in the bush, and in the desert lands.

This is a song from western Africa that tells about the joy of making music.

Ye Jaliya Da

Folk Song from West Africa

Percussion Introduction

Ye ja - li - ya da _____ Al - lah le - ka ja - li - ya da.

Ye ja - li - ya da _____ Al - lah le - ka ja - li - ya da.

le - ka ja - li - ya da.

© DWADD. Used by permission.

In western Africa, a plucked string instrument called the *kora* is especially popular among the Mandingo and Wolof of Senegal and Gambia and the Malinke of the Republic of Guinea. Listen to how the *kora* is played in this piece.

Jula Faso ....Jobarteh

Add a Percussion Part

Practice playing one of these rhythm patterns.
Then play it as an accompaniment to "Ye Jaliya Da."

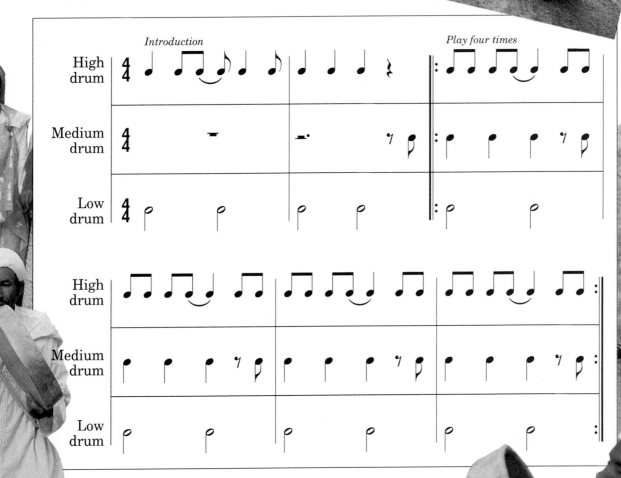

The great religious and political leader Mahatma Gandhi used this prayer-song at his daily prayer meetings. The words speak about God giving wisdom to everyone. Gandhi paid respect to all religions. *Ishware is* what the Hindus call God. *Allah* is what the Moslems call God.

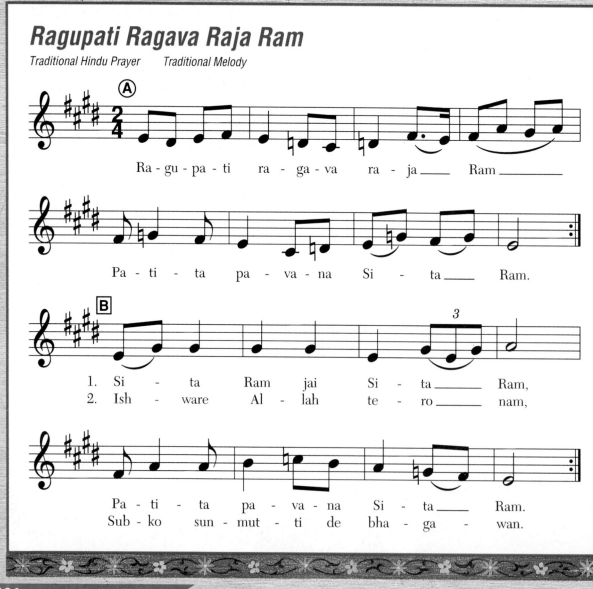

Ragupati Ragava Raja Ram

Traditional Hindu Prayer   *Traditional Melody*

Ⓐ Ra - gu - pa - ti   ra - ga - va   ra - ja____ Ram____

Pa - ti - ta   pa - va - na   Si - ta____ Ram.

Ⓑ
1. Si - ta   Ram   jai   Si - ta_____ Ram,
2. Ish - ware   Al - lah   te - ro_____ nam,

Pa - ti - ta   pa - va - na   Si - ta____ Ram.
Sub - ko   sun - mut - ti   de   bha - ga - wan.

The instrument most associated with the sound of India is the *sitar*. The *sitar* is used mainly for playing classical Indian music. Traditional Indian music is not written down but is taught by the master player to the pupil. The music is based on age-old patterns and traditions, and there is much improvisation in this style.

The *sitar* has been made popular by the great player Ravi Shankar. Listen to him as he performs this piece.

Dadra (excerpt)...............Traditional Indian

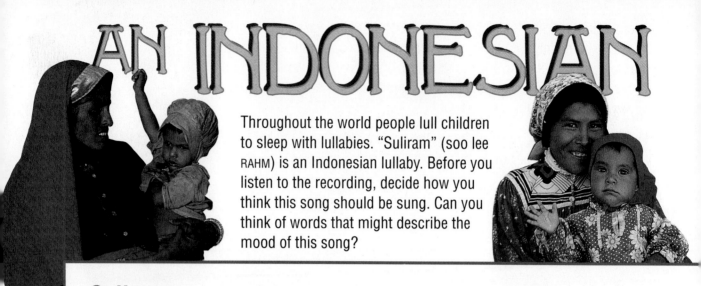

AN INDONESIAN

Throughout the world people lull children to sleep with lullabies. "Suliram" (soo lee RAHM) is an Indonesian lullaby. Before you listen to the recording, decide how you think this song should be sung. Can you think of words that might describe the mood of this song?

Suliram

English Words by Marc Merson   *Folk Song from Indonesia*

Su - li - ram, Su - li - ram, ram, ram, Su - li - ram,

rest now, my child.   As the earth a - waits the cool-ing show - er,

So sleep is wait-ing, for you, my lit-tle flow - er, Su - li - one.

Shad - ows are tempt - ing, They want you to play.

A New Moon

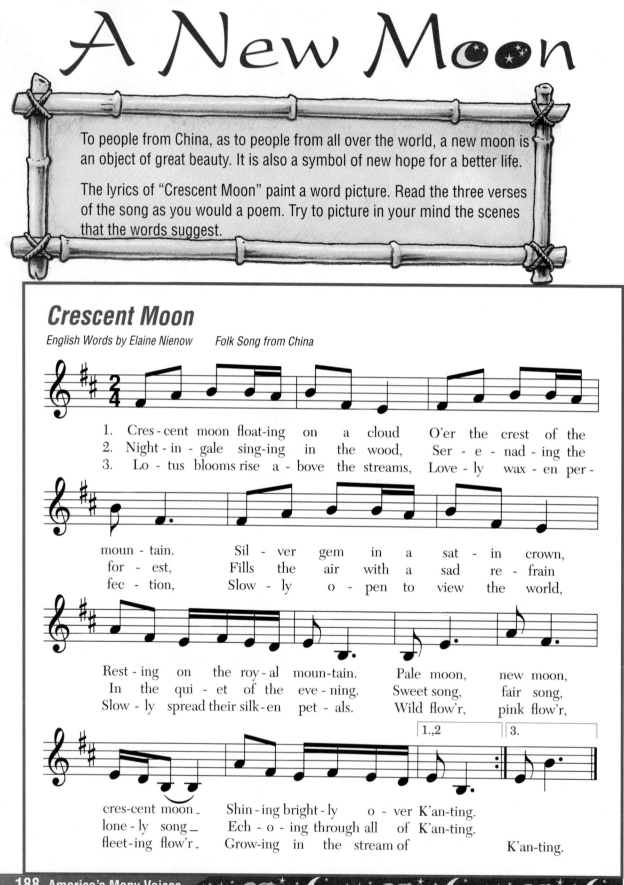

To people from China, as to people from all over the world, a new moon is an object of great beauty. It is also a symbol of new hope for a better life.

The lyrics of "Crescent Moon" paint a word picture. Read the three verses of the song as you would a poem. Try to picture in your mind the scenes that the words suggest.

Crescent Moon

English Words by Elaine Nienow   *Folk Song from China*

1. Cres - cent moon float-ing   on   a   cloud   O'er the crest of the
2. Night - in - gale sing-ing   in   the wood,   Ser - e - nad - ing the
3. Lo - tus blooms rise a - bove the streams,   Love - ly   wax - en per -

moun - tain.   Sil - ver   gem   in   a   sat - in   crown,
for - est,   Fills   the   air   with   a   sad   re - frain
fec - tion,   Slow - ly   o - pen   to   view   the   world,

Rest - ing   on   the roy - al   moun-tain.   Pale moon,   new moon,
In   the   qui - et of the   eve - ning.   Sweet song,   fair song,
Slow - ly   spread their silk-en   pet - als.   Wild flow'r,   pink flow'r,

cres-cent moon _   Shin - ing bright - ly   o - ver K'an-ting.
lone - ly song _   Ech - o - ing through all   of K'an-ting.
fleet-ing flow'r _   Grow-ing   in   the stream of   K'an-ting.

Play an Accompaniment

Accompany the song on the autoharp. Press both the D₇ and the D minor buttons at the same time. This will cause the felt dampers to silence all the strings except the D's and A's. Strum on the first beat of each measure.

You can play this bell ostinato all through the song.

In a Retreat Among Bamboos

Leaning alone in
the close bamboos,
I am playing my lute
and humming a song
Too softly for
anyone to hear—
Except my comrade,
the bright moon

Wang Wei

The Poet Lin Bu Wandering in the Moonlight   *Du Jin*

Hanging scroll, ink and slight color on paper, h. 156.5. Du Jin, Chinese, active ca. 1465-1505, Ming Dynasty. © The Cleveland Museum of Art, John L. Sevrance Fund, 54.582.

WINTER WINDS

The islands that comprise Japan stretch for over a thousand miles from the northeast to the southwest. The southern areas are very warm, but in the north, the winds that originate in Siberia can be bitter cold. These winds often bring several feet of snow to the northern areas.

Learn to sing this song from Japan. It has only three different notes. Can you learn to play it on bells or recorder?

Biting Wind   (Ōsamu Kosamu)

English Words by Gloria J. Kiester   *Folk Song from Japan*

1
Bit-ing wind,   bit-ing cold; _____
Ō - sa-mu, ko-sa-mu, _____

2
Child-ren of the moun-tains are cry-ing from the cold; _
Ya - ma-ka-ra   ko - zoo ga na - i - te - ki-ta _____

Japanese Folk Song. Translation © 1993 Gloria J. Kiester, Used by permission.

Why are they cry-ing, cry-ing from the cold? _____
na - n to it - te na - i - te - ki - ta? _____

"We are in the wind; it's bit-ter, bit-ter cold!"
"Sa-mu-i to it - te na - i - te - ki - ta!"

Bit - ing wind, bit - ing cold. _____
Ō - sa - mu ko - sa - mu. _____

Bit - ing cold. _____
Ko - sa - mu. _____

EARLIEST AMERICANS

Noh ay loh ah noh ay loh ah

Wah ah day oh nah wee yahn nah lay

Ah _____ day oh nah wee yahn nah lay

Nah yah nah ah wee oh _____ mee tehn lah lay

Nah yah nah ah wee oh _____ mee tehn lah lay _____

Songs and dances are of great importance in the ceremonies and rituals of Native Americans. Chester Mahooty of the American Indian Dance Theater sings "Zuni Sunrise Call," a song sung at sunrise to greet the beginning of a new day.

Listen as R. Carlos Nakai, a gifted Native American, plays a variation of the traditional Zuni melody on his hand-crafted wooden flute. Can you think of words to describe this music?

 Zuni Song ....R. Carlos Nakai

A SONG OF THE AMERICAN REVOLUTION

"Yankee Doodle" is the most famous song to come out of the American Revolution. But "Johnny Has Gone for a Soldier" is probably the most beautiful.

As you listen to the recording, imagine the sadness felt by a young woman when her loved one went to fight in the war.

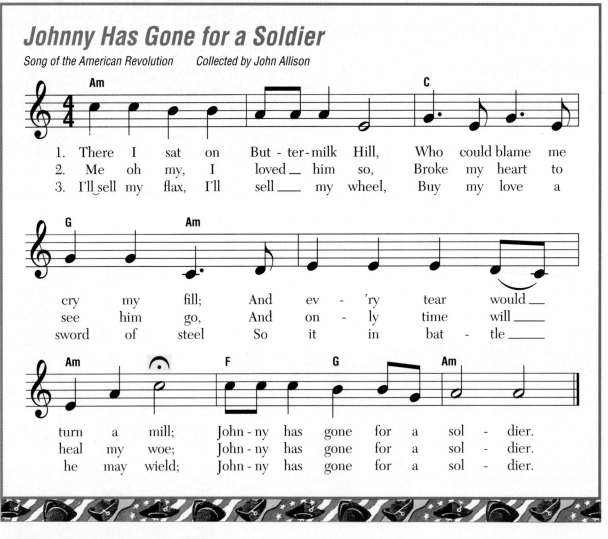

Johnny Has Gone for a Soldier

Song of the American Revolution   *Collected by John Allison*

1. There I sat on But-ter-milk Hill, Who could blame me
2. Me oh my, I loved him so, Broke my heart to
3. I'll sell my flax, I'll sell my wheel, Buy my love a

cry my fill; And ev-'ry tear would
see him go, And on-ly time will
sword of steel So it in bat-tle

turn a mill; John-ny has gone for a sol - dier.
heal my woe; John-ny has gone for a sol - dier.
he may wield; John-ny has gone for a sol - dier.

Oil on canvas. H.149 in. W. 255 in. The Metropolitan Museum of Art, Gift of John Stewart Kennedy, 1897. (97.34).

Washington Crossing the Delaware   *Emanuel Gottlieb Leutze*

Washington

He played by the river when he was young,
He raced with rabbits along the hills,
He fished for minnows, and climbed and swung,
And hooted back at the whippoorwills.
Strong and slender and tall he grew—
and then, one morning, the bugles blew.

Over the hills the summons came,
Over the river's shining rim.
He said that his country needed him,
And he answered, "Coming!" and marched away
For many a night and many a day.

Perhaps when the marches were hot and long
He'd think of the river flowing by
Or, camping under the winter sky,
Would hear the whippoorwill's far–off song.
Boy or soldier, in peace or strife,
He loved America all his life!

Nancy Byrd Turner

The following resolution was presented to the House of Representatives on the death of our first President.

To the memory of the man, first in war, first in peace, and first in the hearts of his countrymen.

A CIVIL WAR SONG

"Battle Cry of Freedom" was a very popular rallying song of the North. Soldiers sang it in battle, in camps, and on long marches. The Confederates were also attracted to this spirited tune and had a version of their own. Here is one verse of the Northern version and one verse of the Southern version.

Battle Cry of Freedom

Northern Words by George F. Root   *Southern Words by W. H. Barnes*   *Music by George F. Root*

Ⓐ **VERSE**

(Northern) Yes, we'll ral - ly round the flag, boys, we'll ral - ly once a - gain,
(Southern) Our __ gal - lant boys have marched to the roll - ing of the drums,

Shout - ing the bat - tle cry of free - dom,
Shout, shout, the bat - tle cry of free - dom,

We will ral - ly from the hill - side, we'll gath - er from the plain,
Be - neath it oft we've conquered and will con-quer oft a - gain,

Shout - ing the bat - tle cry of free - dom.
Shout, shout, the bat - tle cry of free - dom.

Black soldiers at Camp during Civil War   *William Penn*

B REFRAIN

G

The   Un - ion   for - ev - er,   Hur - rah,   boys,   Hur-rah!
Our   Dix - ie   for - ev - er,   she's   never   at   a   loss.

G   D₇

Down   with   the   trai - tor,   Up   with   the   star;
Down   with   the   eag - le and   up   with   the   cross;

G   C

While we   ral - ly round the flag,   boys,   ral - ly   once   a-gain,
We'll __   ral - ly round the bonny flag,   we'll   ral - ly   once   a-gain,

G   D₇   G

Shout - ing   the   bat - tle   cry   of   free - dom.
Shout,   shout   the   bat - tle   cry   of   free - dom.

SINGING

FOR FREEDOM

As you listen to the recording of "Oh, Freedom," notice the vocal tone color of the singers. Who is singing?

Odetta, a well-known African American folk singer and guitarist, has been an important interpreter of African American music since the 1950s. How is her version of these spirituals different from the version in your book?

Oh, Freedom and *Come and Go with Me*
................African American Spirituals

Oh, Freedom

African American Spiritual

1. Oh, _____ free - dom! Oh, _____ free - dom!
2. No more cry - in', No more cry - in',
3. There'll be sing - in', There'll be sing - in',
4. Oh, _____ free - dom! Oh, _____ free - dom!

Oh, _____ free - dom o - ver me. _____
No more cry - in' o - ver me! _____
There'll be sing - in' o - ver me! _____
Oh, _____ free - dom o - ver me! _____

And be - fore I'd be a slave, I'll be bur - ied in my grave,

And go home to my Lord and be free. _____

MUSIC with a MESSAGE

The composer of this song, Bob Dylan, is well known not only for his song-writing, but for his performances. Dylan was a part of the folk music sound in the 1960s. Later, he played electric guitar with his folk-songs, and a whole new sound was born.

Many of Dylan's songs have a message. Do you know what the message of this song is?

Blowin' in the Wind

Words and Music by Bob Dylan

1. How man-y roads must a man walk down be-fore they
2. How man-y years must a moun-tain ex-ist be-fore it is
3. How man-y times must a man look up be-fore he can

call him a man? How man-y seas must a white dove sail be-
washed to the sea? How man-y years can some peo-ple ex-ist be-
see the sky? How man-y ears must one man have be-

fore she sleeps in the sand? How man-y times must the
fore they're al-lowed to be free? How man-y times can a
fore he can hear peo-ple cry? How man-y deaths will it

can-non balls fly be-fore they're for-ev-er banned?
man turn his head and pre-tend that he just does-n't see?
take till he knows that too man-y peo-ple have died?

} The

an-swer, my friend, is blow-in' in the wind, The an-swer is blow-in' in the

1.,2.
3.

wind. wind. The an-swer is blow-in' in the wind.

Folk Music in the Making

Like many folk singers, Cisco Houston spent a lot of time traveling around the country in search of new songs. It seems likely that this song was written during one of the long and lonely trips that took Houston far away from home.

How do the words of "Nine Hundred Miles" describe the feelings of someone who is far from home?

Nine Hundred Miles

African American Work Song   *Arranged and Adapted by Cisco Houston*

1. I am rid-in' on this train, There are tears in __ my eyes,
2. Well, this train __ I ride on Is a hundred coach-es long.
3. Well, I'll pawn __ you my watch And I'll pawn you __ my chain.

And I'm tryin' to read a let-ter from my home. _____
You can hear the whis-tle blow a hun-dred miles. _____
I'll ____ pawn __ you my gold __ dia-mond ring. _____

If this train runs me right, I'll be home Sat-ur-day night,
And the lonesome whis-tle call Is the mournful-est __ of all,
For if this train runs me right, I'll be home Sat-ur-day night,

For I'm nine hun-dred miles from _ my home. _____
'Cause it's nine hun-dred miles from _ my home. _____
For I'm nine hun-dred miles from _ my home. _____

Folk Songs of Tomorrow

The songs that folk singers make up today are recorded and are played on radio and television, so that people all over the world hear and sing each other's tunes. Those you remember and sing often will be the folk songs of tomorrow.

On this recording, you will hear a group called The Byrds singing a special arrangement of Stephen Foster's hit song *Oh, Susanna.*

 Oh, Susanna ....Stephen Foster

In this song, someone offers a friend a place to sleep. Maybe one day the favor will be returned.

Listen to Carole King perform a song she wrote about friendship. How is the message of this song like that of "Pallet on the Floor"?

You've Got a Friend (excerpt)
...................Carole King

Pallet on the Floor

Traditional

REFRAIN **B♭**

You made me a pal - let on — the floor, Yes, you

B♭ **F**

made me a pal - let on — the floor, When I

F **A₇** **Dm** **G₇**

had no place to go, — You o - pened up your door, —

F **C₇** **F** *Fine*

And you ⁊ made me a pal - let on — the floor.

Add a Harmony Part

Here is a countermelody to sing with the refrain of "Pallet on the Floor."

Countermelody (**REFRAIN**)

You made me a pal - let on the floor,

Made me a pal - let on the floor,

Had no place to go, — you o - pened up your door, —

And you made me a pal - let on — the floor.

VERSE

1. Oh, I was sad and so dis - sat - is - fied, Yes,
2. Oh, I won't come a - round here an - y - more, No,
3. So don't — turn a good friend from your home, No,

I was sad and so dis - sat - is - fied; I was
I won't come a - round here an - y - more; But —
don't — turn a good friend from your home, For —

sad and dis - sat - is - fied that I near - ly cried,
if — I ev - er do — it'll be be - cause of you,
may - be there'll come a day — that you will roam,

D.C. al Fine

Then you made me a pal - let on — the floor.
'Cause you made me a pal - let on — the floor.
And be looking for a pal - let on — the floor.

Pete Seeger
FOLK SINGER AND COMPOSER

The Weavers performing at Carnegie Hall, November, 1980.

"Turn, Turn, Turn" was written by Pete Seeger, one of America's most famous folk singers. Follow the music as you listen to the recording. Join in on Section A when you can.

Turn, Turn, Turn (To Everything There Is a Season)

Words from the Book of Ecclesiastes   *Adaptation and Music by Pete Seeger*

To ev-'ry - thing, (Turn, turn, turn) There is a sea-son (Turn, turn, turn) And a time for ev - 'ry pur-pose un - der heav - en.

1. A time to be born, a time to die; A time to
2. A time to build up, a time to break down; A time to
3. A time of ___ love, a time of hate; A time of
4. A time to ___ gain, a time to lose; A time to

A Countermelody for Section B

Melody: A time to be born, a time to die; A time to plant, a time to

Countermelody: Turn, Turn, Turn, Turn, Turn,

reap; A time to kill, a time to heal; A time to laugh, a time to weep.

Turn, Turn, Turn, Turn, Turn, Turn, Turn.

Pete Seeger was the founding member of a very famous folk group—The Weavers. Listen as they perform a well-known song written by another famous songwriter—Woody Guthrie.

So Long, It's Been Good to Know You............Woody Guthrie

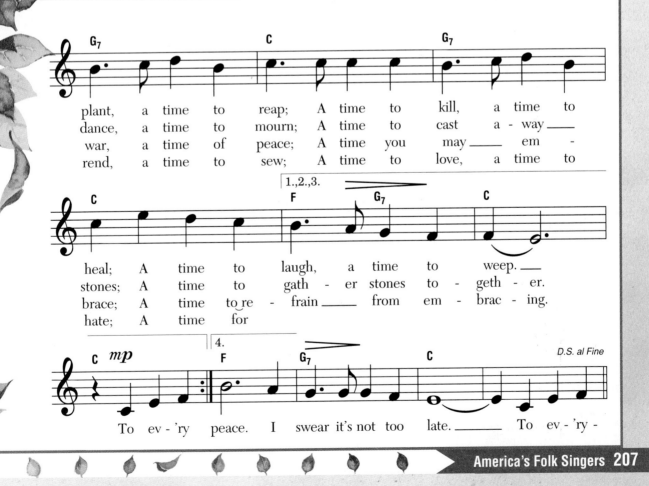

plant, a time to reap; A time to kill, a time to
dance, a time to mourn; A time to cast a - way___
war, a time of peace; A time you may ___ em -
rend, a time to sew; A time to love, a time to

1.,2.,3.

heal; A time to laugh, a time to weep.___
stones; A time to gath - er stones to - geth - er.
brace; A time to re - frain ___ from em - brac - ing.
hate; A time for

4.

To ev - 'ry peace. I swear it's not too late. ___ To ev - 'ry-

THUNDER ON THE

A great deal of folklore is associated with American railroads. Some of the stories told about the Wabash Cannon Ball are totally outrageous. In one version, the train is so fast that it arrives at its destination before it leaves its starting place!

Follow the words as you listen to the song. Can you find the words that describe the sound of this mighty train?

Wabash Cannon Ball

Traditional

Ⓐ VERSE

1. From the coast of the At - lan - tic to the wide Pa - cif - ic
2. There are name of great im - por - tance that is known by one and
2. There are ci - ties of im - por - tance that are reached a - long the
   Spring-field and De - ca - tur and Pe - or - ia, Mon - tre -

shore, From the warm and sun - ny South - land to the
all, It's the West - ern com - bi - na - tion called the
way, Chi - ca - go and Saint Lou - is and Rock
al, On the West - ern com - bi - na - tion called the

1.
isle of La - bra - dor, There's a Wa - bash Can-non Ball.

Is - land, San - ta Fe, And

RAILS

B **REFRAIN**

Just lis-ten to the jin-gle, the rum-ble, and the roar Of the
might-y lo-co-mo-tive as she streams a-long the shore, Hear the
thun-der of the en-gine, hear the lone-some whis-tle call, It's the
West-ern com-bi-na-tion called the Wa-bash Can-non Ball.

MIKE REID
COMPOSER AND PERFORMER

On this recording, Mike Reid talks about his career in music.

Careers in Music—Mike Reid

Mike Reid is both the composer and performer of this song about the love of home.

Turning for Home ....Mike Reid

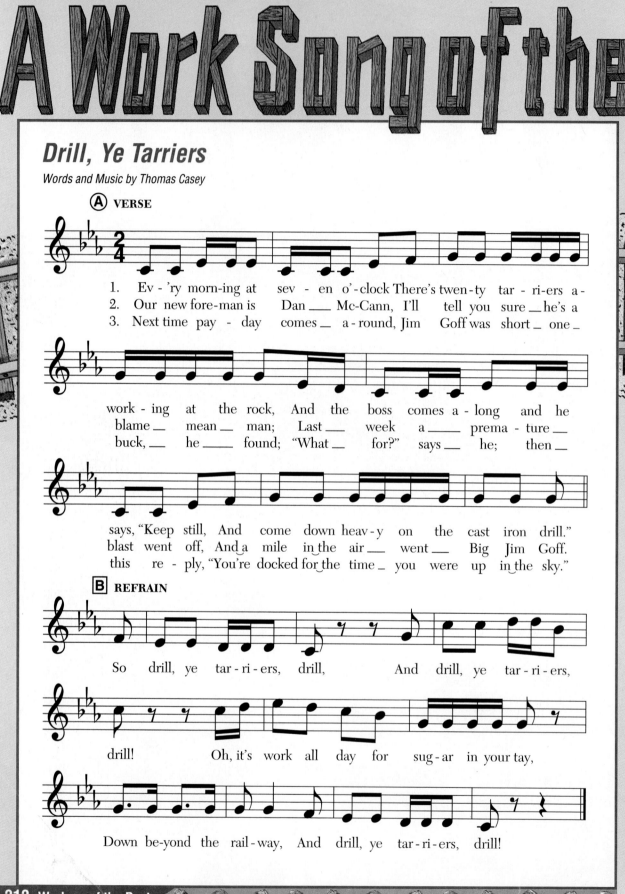

Drill, Ye Tarriers

Words and Music by Thomas Casey

A VERSE

1. Ev-'ry morn-ing at sev-en o'-clock There's twen-ty tar-ri-ers a-
2. Our new fore-man is Dan ___ Mc-Cann, I'll tell you sure ___ he's a
3. Next time pay-day comes ___ a-round, Jim Goff was short ___ one ___

work-ing at the rock, And the boss comes a-long and he
blame ___ mean ___ man; Last ___ week a ___ prema-ture ___
buck, ___ he ___ found; "What ___ for?" says ___ he; then ___

says, "Keep still, And come down heav-y on the cast iron drill."
blast went off, And a mile in the air ___ went ___ Big Jim Goff.
this re-ply, "You're docked for the time ___ you were up in the sky."

B REFRAIN

So drill, ye tar-ri-ers, drill, And drill, ye tar-ri-ers,

drill! Oh, it's work all day for sug-ar in your tay,

Down be-yond the rail-way, And drill, ye tar-ri-ers, drill!

RAILROAD

In the 1880s, much of the work on the building of American railroads was done by Irishmen, then called *tarriers*. These workers dug and blasted out the right of way for the railroads, east and west. This humorous song tells of the hardships of their rock-drilling vocation.

Add an Ostinato

This added part may be repeated throughout the refrain.

Drill, ye tar - ri - ers, drill.

Listen to this song, which pays tribute to some workers of today. It is sung by the popular group Alabama. Can you list the occupations that are mentioned in the song?

Forty Hour Week.................Dave Loggins, Lisa Silvers, and Don Schlitz

A FOLK HERO

His Hammer in His Hand   *Palmer C. Hayden*

John Henry, a legendary character,
was the southern steel-driving man
whose fame spread across the country.
He thought the strength of his arm was
superior to that of a mechanical steam drill.

This song is a **ballad**—a song that tells a story.
Let your voice express the meaning of the words.

John Henry

Folk Song from Southern United States

1. When John Hen - ry _____ was just a lit - tle ba - by,
2. Well, the cap - tain _____ said to John _ Hen - ry,
3. John _ Hen - ry _____ told _ his _____ cap - tain,
4. Oh, the man that _ in - vent - ed the _____ steam _ drill,

Sit - tin' on his dad - dy's knee,
"Gon - na bring that steam drill round,
"Well, a man ain't nothin' but a man,
He _____ thought that he was mighty fine,

He _____ gave one long and _____ lone - some cry,
Gon - na take that steam drill _____ out on the job,
But be - fore I let your steam drill beat me down,
But John Hen - ry drove his steel _____ fif - teen feet,

Said, "A ham - mer be the death of me."   me."
Gon - na whop that steel _____ on _____ down."   down."
I'll _____ die with a ham - mer in my hand."   hand."
And the steam drill drove _____ on - ly nine.   nine.

5. John Henry kept hammerin' on the mountain,
   There was lightnin' in his eye.
   He drove so hard that he broke his heart,
   And he laid down his hammer and he died. *(2 times)*

6. They carried him off to the graveyard,
   They buried him in the sand.
   And people came from near and far
   To praise that steel-drivin' man. *(2 times)*

Life on the Sea

The "Jamestown" Homeward Bound

Forecastle Shanty from the United States

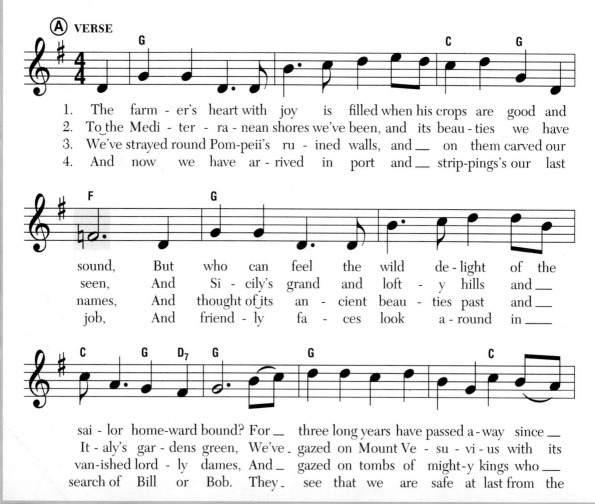

A VERSE

G   C   G

1. The farm-er's heart with joy is filled when his crops are good and
2. To the Medi-ter-ra-nean shores we've been, and its beau-ties we have
3. We've strayed round Pom-peii's ru-ined walls, and — on them carved our
4. And now we have ar-rived in port and — strip-pings's our last

F   G

sound, But who can feel the wild de-light of the
seen, And Si-cily's grand and loft-y hills and —
names, And thought of its an-cient beau-ties past and —
job, And friend-ly fa-ces look a-round in —

C   G   D₇   G   G   C

sai-lor home-ward bound? For — three long years have passed a-way since —
It-aly's gar-dens green, We've-gazed on Mount Ve-su-vi-us with its
van-ished lord-ly dames, And — gazed on tombs of might-y kings who —
search of Bill or Bob. They — see that we are safe at last from the

This song was a favorite of sailors in bygone days. Built in 1844, the *Jamestown* was a sloop of war. Her claim to fame was to be sent by the United States government to Ireland as a relief ship to aid the victims of the famine of 1847.

Notice in the song that the sailors sing of cruising "up the Straits." This was the nickname used for sailing the Mediterranean Sea. What specific sights did the men remember from this trip? Describe the feelings of the sailors at this point in their journey.

we left free-dom's shore, Our _____ long - felt wish has come at last, and we're
rag-ged slum-bering dome; Night _____ is the time in that red clime when the
oft in bat - tle won, But _____ what were they all in their sway with _____
per-ils of the sea, Saying, "You're wel-come Co-lum-bia's mar - i - ners, to _____

B REFRAIN

home - ward bound once _ more. To _ where the sky is clear as the
sai - lor thinks of _ home. So _ fill _ our _ sails with the
our brave Wash - ing - ton?
homes and lib - er - ty."

maid - en's eye who _ longs for our re - turn, To the
fav - oring gales, and with ship - mates all a - round, We'll _

land where milk and hon - ey flows and _ lib - er - ty was _ born.
give three cheers for our star - ry flag and the *James-town* home-ward _ bound.

Casey Jones

Words by T. Lawrence Seibert   *Music by Eddie Newton*

B♭

1. Come, all you round-ers, if you want to hear
2. Put in your wa-ter and shov-el your coal,
3. Ca-sey pulled up at Re-no hill,

B♭   **F₇**

A sto-ry a-bout a brave en-gi-neer,
Put your head out the win-dow, watch them driv-ers roll,
He too-ted for the cross-ing with an aw-ful shrill,

B♭

And Ca-sey Jones was the round-er's name,
I'll run her till she leaves the rail,
The switch-man knew by the en-gine's moan

B♭   **F₇**   **B♭**

On a six eight wheel-er, boys, he won his fame.
'Cause I'm eight hours late with that West-ern mail.
That the man at the throt-tle was Ca-sey Jones.

B♭

The call-er called Ca-sey at a half past four.
He looked at his watch and his watch was slow,
He pulled up with-in two miles of the place,

B♭   **F₇**

Ca-sey kissed his wife at the sta-tion door,
He looked at the wa-ter and the wa-ter was low,
And Num-ber Four stared him in the face,

Casey Jones was known for the speed at which he could make a train travel and for the wonderful sound he could get out of the train whistle. Some stories tell us that the people who worked in the fields near the railroad track could tell when Casey was at the throttle by the sound of the train whistle.

He mount - ed to the cab - in with his or - ders in his hand,
He turned __ to the fire - man and then __ he __ said,
He turned __ to the fire - man, said, "Boy, you bet - ter jump,

And he took his fare - well trip __ to the Prom - ised Land."
"We're __ goin' to reach __ Fris - co, but we'll all __ be dead."
'Cause there's two __ lo - co - mo - tives that's a - go - in' to bump."

REFRAIN

Ca - sey Jones, __
Mount - ed to the cab - in,
Goin' to reach __ Fris - co,
Two __ lo - co - mo - tives,

Ca - sey Jones, __
With his or - ders in his hands,
But we'll all __ be __ dead,
That's a - go - in' to __ bump,

Ca - sey Jones, __
Mount - ed to the cab - in,
Goin' to reach __ Fris - co,
Two __ lo - co - mo - tives,

And he took his fare - well trip __ to the Prom - ised Land.
We're __ goin' to reach __ Fris - co, but we'll all __ be dead.
There's __ two __ lo - co - mo - tives that's a - go - in' to bump.

Many of the patriotic songs we sing have been around for a long time. Present-day composers, such as the composer of this song, also write about love of country.

The Voices of Pride

Words and Music by Ned Ginsburg

I hear A - mer-i - ca sing - ing; I hear the voic-es of pride

call-ing out all through the na - tion, It's a ris - ing tide.

I see the flags all un-furl - ing, and then, the ban-ners in hand, _

During the War of 1812, Francis Scott Key wrote the words of this song after spending an anxious night awaiting the outcome of an enemy bombardment at Fort McHenry. However, it was not until 1931 that an act of Congress established "The Star-Spangled Banner" as the national anthem of the United States.

Listen to another recording of our national anthem. What is different about the interpretation? Is the meter the same?

The Star-Spangled Banner ....Francis Scott Key and John Stafford Smith

The Star-Spangled Banner

Words by Francis Scott Key   Music by John Stafford Smith

1. Oh, __ say! can you see, by the dawn's ear-ly light, What so
2. On the shore, dim-ly seen through the mists of the deep, Where the
3. Oh, __ thus be it ever when __ free men shall stand Be -

proud-ly we hailed at the twi-light's last gleam-ing, Whose broad
foe's haugh-ty host in dread si-lence re-pos-es, What is
tween their loved homes and the war's des-o-la-tion! Blest with

stripes and bright stars, through the per-il-ous fight, O'er the
that which the breeze, o'er the tow-er-ing steep, As it
vict-'ry and peace, may the heav'n-res-cued land Praise the

ram-parts we watched were so gal-lant-ly stream-ing? And the
fit-ful-ly blows, half con-ceals, half dis-clos-es? Now it
Pow'r that hath made and pre-served us a na-tion! Then __

The Peale Museum, Baltimore City Life Museums.

By Dawn's Early Light   *E. Percy Moran 1912*

rock - ets' red glare, the bombs burst - ing in air, Gave
catch - es the gleam of the morn - ing's first beam, In full
con - quer we must, for our cause it is just, And

proof through the night that our flag was still there. Oh,
glo - ry re - flected now __ shines on the stream; 'Tis the
this be our motto: "In __ God is our trust!" And the

say, does that __ Star-Span-gled Ban - ner __ yet __ wave __ O'er the
Star-Span - gled __ Ban - ner, oh, long may __ it __ wave __ O'er the
Star-Span - gled __ Ban - ner in tri - umph shall __ wave __ O'er the

land ____ of the free and the home of the brave?
land ____ of the free and the home of the brave!
land ____ of the free and the home of the brave!

LET FREEDOM RING

Samuel Francis Smith was inspired to write the words of this well-known patriotic hymn while he was still a young student. A group of schoolchildren gave the first performance of "America" in Boston, Massachusetts, on July 4, 1832.

America

Words by Samuel Francis Smith   *Traditional Melody*

1. My coun - try! 'tis of thee, Sweet land of
2. My na - tive coun - try, thee, Land of the
3. Let mu - sic swell the breeze, And ring from
4. Our fa - thers' God, to Thee, Au - thor of

lib - er - ty, Of thee I sing; Land where my
no - ble free, Thy name I love; I love thy
all the trees Sweet Free - dom's song; Let mor - tal
lib - er - ty, To Thee we sing; Long may our

fa - thers died, Land of the Pil - grims' pride,
rocks and rills, Thy woods and tem - pled hills,
tongues a - wake, Let all that breathe par - take,
land be bright With Free - dom's ho - ly light;

From ev - 'ry ___ moun - tain - side, Let ___ free - dom ring!
My heart ___ with ___ rap - ture thrills Like ___ that a - bove.
Let rocks ___ their ___ si - lence break, The ___ sound pro - long.
Pro - tect ___ us ___ by Thy might, Great ___ God, our King!

A VIEW OF AMERICA

One day in 1893, Katharine Lee Bates stood on the top of Colorado's Pikes Peak and looked for miles in every direction. She seemed to be seeing all of America—mountains, valleys, wide prairies. It was after this experience that she wrote the poem "America, the Beautiful."

America, the Beautiful

Words by Katharine Lee Bates   Music by Samuel A. Ward

1. O beau - ti - ful for spa - cious skies, For am - ber waves of grain,
2. O beau - ti - ful for Pil - grim feet, Whose stern im - pas-sioned stress
3. O beau - ti - ful for pa - triot dream That sees, be - yond the years,

For pur - ple moun-tain maj - es - ties A - bove the fruit - ed plain!
A thor - ough-fare for free - dom beat A - cross the wil - der - ness!
Thine al - a - bas - ter cit - ies gleam, Un - dimmed by hu - man tears!

A - mer - i - ca! A - mer - i - ca! God shed His grace on thee,
A - mer - i - ca! A - mer - i - ca! God mend thine ev - 'ry flaw,
A - mer - i - ca! A - mer - i - ca! God shed His grace on thee,

And crown thy good with broth - er-hood, From sea to shin - ing sea!
Con - firm thy soul in self con-trol, Thy lib - er - ty in law!
And crown thy good with broth - er-hood, From sea to shin - ing sea!

An African American group sings this rousing gospel version of *America, the Beautiful.*

America, the Beautiful.............Katharine Lee Bates and Samuel A. Ward

In November, 1861, Julia Ward Howe, a prominent writer and pioneer of women's rights, and her husband visited a Union army camp near Washington, D.C. While there, they joined the soldiers in singing the popular marching song "John Brown's Body." A friend suggested she write new words for the song. She titled her poem "Battle Hymn of the Republic," and it has gone on to become one of our most loved and widely sung patriotic songs.

Battle Hymn of the Republic

Words by Julia Ward Howe   Music by William Steffe

A VERSE

1. Mine ___ eyes have seen the glo - ry of the
2. He has sound - ed forth the trum - pet that shall

com - ing of the Lord; He is tramp - ling out the vin - tage
nev - er call re - treat; He is sift - ing out the hearts of

where the grapes of wrath are stored; He hath
men be - fore the judg - ment seat. Oh, be

loosed the fate - ful light - ning of His ter - ri - ble swift sword;
swift, my soul, to an - swer Him! Be ju - bi - lant, my feet!

His truth is march - ing on.
Our God is march - ing on.

SONG

Lift Every Voice

The words of this stirring song were written in 1900 by the poet James Weldon Johnson to commemorate the birthday of Abraham Lincoln. The words were set to music by J. Rosamond Johnson, the poet's brother. "Lift Ev'ry Voice and Sing" is regarded as the African American national anthem.

Lift Ev'ry Voice and Sing

Words by James Weldon Johnson   Music by J. Rosamond Johnson

1. Lift ev'ry voice and sing, till earth and heav-en ring,
2. Ston-y the road we trod, bit-ter the chas-t'ning rod

Ring with the har-mo-nies of lib — er-ty.
Felt in the days when hope un — born ____ had died.

Let our re-joic-ing rise high as the lis-t'ning ____ skies,
Yet with a stead-y beat have not our wea-ry ____ feet

Let it re-sound loud as the roll — ing sea.
Come to the place for which our fa — thers died.

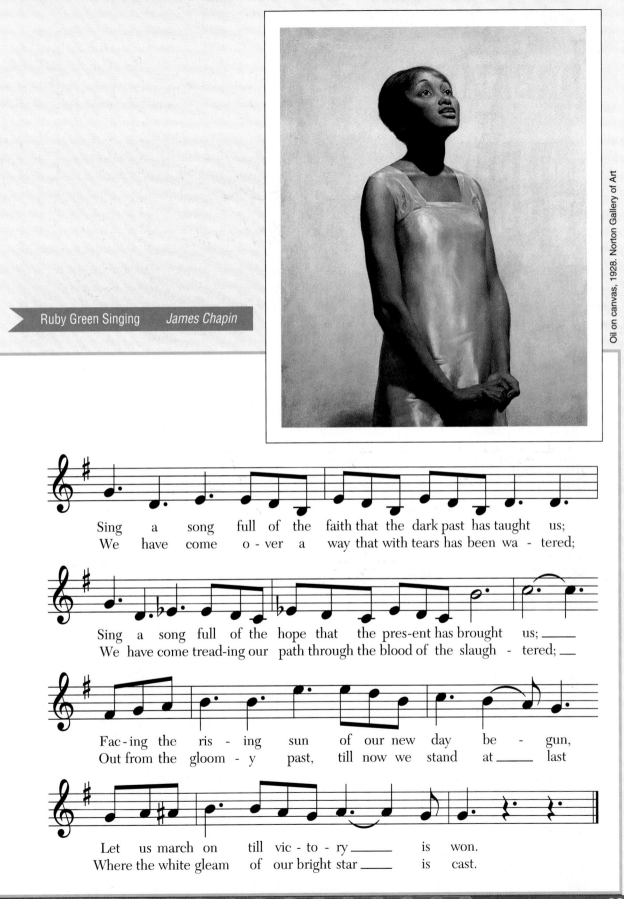

Ruby Green Singing   *James Chapin*

Oil on canvas, 1928. Norton Gallery of Art

Sing   a   song   full   of   the   faith that the dark past has taught   us;
We   have   come   o - ver   a   way that with tears has been wa - tered;

Sing   a   song full   of   the   hope that   the pres-ent has brought   us; ____
We have come tread-ing our   path through the blood of the slaugh - tered; __

Fac - ing   the   ris - ing   sun   of our new   day   be -   gun,
Out from the gloom - y   past,   till now we   stand   at ____ last

Let   us march on   till   vic - to - ry ____   is   won.
Where the white gleam   of our bright star ____   is   cast.

DREAMING OF FREEDOM

Dr. Martin Luther King in Jefferson County Court House Jail, Birmingham, Alabama, 1967.

This is a song of the civil rights movement of the 1960s. It points up the deter-mination needed to sing in the streets, spend a night in jail, if necessary, and wake up in the morning ready to carry on the work of the freedom movement.

Woke Up This Morning

African American Spiritual

1. Woke up this morn-ing with my mind (my mind it was) stayed __ on free - dom, (oh, well I)
3. Sing - in' and pray - in' with my mind

Woke up this morn-ing with my mind __ stayed __ on free - dom, (oh, well I)
Sing - in' and pray - in' with my mind __

Woke up this morn-ing with my mind (my mind it was) stayed __ on free - dom, Hal-le-
Sing - in' and pray - in' with my mind

lu, hal-le - lu, hal-le - lu, hal-le - lu, hal-le - lu - jah! __

2. Walk walk (doo doo doo) walk walk walk walk with my mind on free-dom,

Walk walk walk walk (a-well-a) walk walk with my mind on free-dom,

(To verse 3) D.C. al Fine

Ah _____ walk walk walk walk

SING FOR

We celebrate United Nations Day on October 24.
Why are the words of this song appropriate to sing on that day?

We Come to Greet You in Peace (Hevenu Shalom Aleichem)

Hebrew Folk Song

We come to greet you in peace, — We come to
He - ve - nu sha - lom a - lei - chem, He - ve - nu

greet you in peace, — We come to greet — you in
sha - lom a - lei - chem, He - ve - nu sha - lom a -

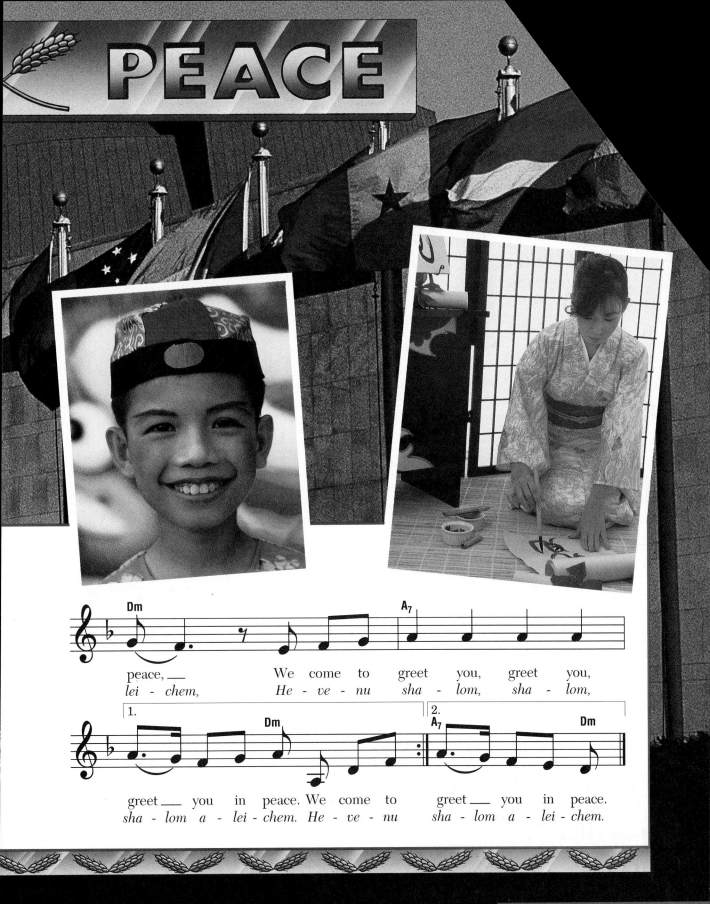

peace, ___ We come to greet you, greet you,
lei - chem, *He - ve - nu* *sha - lom,* *sha - lom,*

greet __ you in peace. We come to greet __ you in peace.
sha - lom a - lei - chem. He - ve - nu sha - lom a - lei - chem.

...song a number of make-believe characters dance on Halloween ...he title of the song tells you about one dance. How many other ...an you identify? Follow the words as you listen to the recording.

When Witches Were Waltzing

Words and Music by Linda Williams

1. One night I went walk-ing out in-to the wood, And
2. I want-ed to watch, so I hid in a tree. I
3. They waltzed in the wood by the light of the stars. The

1. and 2.

found I had wan-dered much more than I should, For I came to a
said to my-self, "Can't be-lieve what I see!" It's a pump-kin
scare-crows were strum-ming their ghost-ly gui-

mea-dow, a ma-gi-cal spot, Where witch-es were waltz-ing. I nev-er for-
polk-a, a gob-lin ga-votte, and witch-es were waltz-ing. I nev-er for-

got. What a wild and weird and won-der-ful sight, When witch-es were

3. and 4. (4. repeats)

waltz-ing on Hal-lo-ween night! -tars For the

Listen for the "skeleton dancers" in this piece for orchestra.
What instruments do you hear?

Danse macabre ....Camille Saint-Saëns

skel - e - ton sam - ba, the mon - ster min-u - et, The pump - kin
witch - es were

1. pol - ka, the gob - lin ga - votte; And
2. waltz - ing, I nev - er for - got What a

wild and weird and won - der - ful sight, When witch - es were

waltz - ing on Hal - lo-ween night!

4.   One day I'll wake up in a wandering mood.
     The West wind will whisper, "Away to the wood!"
     And if you will come with me, we might take a chance,
     We'll dress all in black and join into the dance!
     And we'll all rock and roll while the jack-o-lanterns jitterbug,
     The skeletons samba, the monsters minuet,
     The pumpkins polka, the goblins gavotte.
     I've been there before and I never forgot
     What a wild . . .

Celebrate the Harvest

Fall brings the harvest. It is a time of feasting and celebrating in many countries. In the United States, we have the joyous feast of Thanksgiving.

Come, Ye Thankful People, Come

Words by Henry Alford   Music by George J. Elvey

1. Come, ye thank-ful peo-ple, come, Raise the song of
2. All the bless-ings of the field, All the stores the

har-vest home; All is safe-ly gath-ered in Ere the
gar-dens yield; All the fruits in full sup-ply, Rip-ened

win-ter storms be-gin; God, our Mak-er, doth pro-vide
'neath the sum-mer sky; All that spring with boun-teous hand

Guatemalan Corn Dance. National Dance Institute

For our wants to be sup - plied; Come to God's own
Scat - ters o'er the smil - ing land; All that lib - 'ral

tem - ple, come, Raise the song of har - vest home.
au - tumn pours From her rich o'er - flow - ing stores.

A ROCKIN' HOLIDAY SONG

We usually think of jingle bells as something used on an old-fashioned sled. Here is a swinging, updated jingle-bell song that was popular in the late 1950s and early 1960s.

Jingle-Bell Rock

Words and Music by J. Beal and J. Boothe

Jin-gle-bell, jin-gle-bell, jin-gle-bell rock,   Jin-gle-bell swing and jin-gle-bells ring.

Snow-in' and blow-in' up bush-els of fun.   Now the jin-gle-hop has be-gun.

Jin-gle-bell, jin-gle-bell, jin-gle-bell rock,   Jin-gle-bells chime in jin-gle-bell time.

Dan-cin' and pran-cin' in Jin-gle-bell Square   in the fros-ty air.

What a bright time, it's the right time to rock the night a-way.

Jin-gle-bell time is a swell time to go glid-in' in a one-horse sleigh.

Gid-dy-ap, jin-gle-horse, pick up your feet, jin-gle a-round the clock;

Mix and min-gle in a jin-gl-in' beat, that's the jin-gle bell rock.

1.

2.

that's the jin-gle-bell, that's the jin-gle-bell rock.

Tap or snap the steady beat as you listen to this rap.

Christmas Gift Rap............John Carter and Mary Kay Beall

Festival of Lights

Words and Music by David Eddleman

A

1. Come and cel - e-brate the Fes - ti - val of Lights,
2. Come and cel - e-brate the mir - a - cle of old,

See the can - dle burn - ing, burn - ing oh, so bright;
Sing a song to praise a peo - ple brave and bold,

See the drey - dl spin - ning, spin - ning out of sight,
Sing a mir - a - cle, the sto - ry that is told,

B

Sing to cel - e-brate these hap - py ho - ly nights.
Bright me - no - rah glow - ing, won - drous to be - hold.

Once there was a lamp a-light with oil e-nough for but one night;
Praise the Mac-ca - be - an name, who saved his land from grief and shame;

Then came the mir - a - cle: for eight full days it burned so bright.
Praise for his vic - to - ry, and lib - er - ty for all pro-claim.

Improvise a tambourine part as you listen to this Chanukah song. Will you tap the instrument, shake it, or will your pattern include both tapping and shaking?

1. Come and cel - e-brate the mir - a - cle of old,

2. Sing the mir - a - cle of old, To

1. Sing a song to praise a peo - ple brave and bold;

2. praise a peo - ple brave and bold;

1. Sing the mir - a - cle, the sto - ry that is told,

2. Here the an - cient sto - ry told, Me -

1. Bright me - no - rah burn - ing won-drous to be - hold.

2. no - rah won - drous to be - hold.

THE FEAST OF LIGHTS

Chanukah, or the Feast of Lights, is one of the winter celebrations. People of the Jewish faith celebrate the Feast of Lights for eight days during the month of December.

A special candelabra, the *menorah*, symbolizes the Feast of Lights. During the eight-day festival, one candle is lighted each day from an extra candle called the *shamas* (the "watchman").

A Song of Always

The temple is clean,
The lamp burns bright;
Judiah the leader,
Has started the light.

The sun shines by days,
And dark is the night;
But always and always
The lamp burns bright.

Efraim Rosenzweig

Rock of Ages

English Words by G. Gottheil   *Traditional Hebrew Melody*

1. Rock of A - ges, let our song Praise Thy sav - ing pow - er;

2. Rock of A - ges, Praise Thy sav - ing pow - er;

1. Thou, a - midst the rag - ing foes, Wast our shel - t'ring tow - er.

2. Thou 'midst rag - ing foes, Our shel - t'ring tow - er.

1. Fu - rious they as - sailed us, But Thine arm a - vailed _____ us,

2. Fu - rious they as - sailed us, But thine arm a - vailed __ us,

1. And Thy word broke their sword When our own strength failed _ us.

2. And Thy word broke their sword When our own strength failed _ us.

Yuletide Carol

Deck the Hall

Traditional Carol from Wales

1. { Deck the hall with boughs of hol - ly, }
   { 'Tis the sea - son to be jol - ly, }
2. { See the blaz - ing Yule be - fore us, }
   { Strike the harp and join the chor - us, }

Fa la la la la la la la la.

Countermelody

Fa la la la la la la.

Don we now our gay ap - par - el,
Fol - low me in mer - ry mea - sure,

One of the Christmas customs that has come down through the centuries is decorating the house with holly and mistletoe. In medieval times in Great Britain, one popular legend held that holly, ivy, yew, and mistletoe shielded the home from winter demons that brought cold and darkness.

"Deck the Hall," an old Welsh song that paints a festive scene of holly, harp, and blazing Yule log, is one of the best-known of all secular Christmas carols. It is sung throughout Great Britain and the United States.

The popular group Mannheim Steamroller plays this festive arrangement of "Deck the Hall."

Deck the Hall ....Traditional Carol from Wales

3. Fast away the old year passes,
    Fa la la la la la la la la.
    Hail the new, ye lads and lasses,
    Fa la la la la la la la la.

    Sing we joyous all together,
    Fa la la la la la la la la.
    Heedless of the wind and weather,
    Fa la la la la la la la la.

A Joyful Sound

This old French carol is known as the "Westminster Carol" in England because it is often sung in the Westminster Chapel.

Listen as the The Texas Boys Choir sings their special arrangement of this carol.

 Angels We Have Heard on High
.............Traditional Carol from France

Angels We Have Heard on High

Traditional Carol from France

1. An - gels we have heard on high, Sweet-ly sing-ing o'er the plains,
2. Shep-herds why this ju - bi-lee? Why your joy-ous songs pro-long?

And the moun-tains in re-ply Ech - o - ing their joy - ous strains.
What the glad-some tid - ings be Which in - spire your heav'n-ly song?

REFRAIN

Glo - ri - a

in ex - cel - sis De - o, Glo -

- ri - a in ex - cel - sis De - o.

A TIME FOR CARING

During the holiday season our attention frequently turns to sharing and caring for others.

A Time for Joy

Words and Music by Don Besig

Christ - mas _____ is a tim[e]

hap - pi-ness for ev - 'ry gi[rl]

fam' - lies, _____ a time for friends. _____ A time for

peace on earth, _____ good will to men. _____ And

Christ - mas _____ is a time to share. _____ It's the chance we

have to show the world we real - ly care. _____ A time to

pray for the peace we're dream - ing of, _____ for the

real joy of Christ - mas is love!

Carol from Catalonia

This melody is more than 500 years old. It comes from a region in the northeastern part of Spain. Its capital is Barcelona, and Catalonians speak their own language, Catalan, as well as Spanish.

Cold December

English Words by Aura Kontra   *Fifteenth-Century Melody from Catalonia*

Ⓐ VERSE

1. Cold De-cem-ber days pro-claim that the year is end - ing.
2. For this night the Child has come, peace to man-kind bring - ing.
3. As the wise-men from the East brought their rich-est trea - sure,

And a great re - splen-dent light toward the earth is bend - ing.
An - gels greet Him in a throng, Joy - ful prais - es sing - ing.
We now cel - e - brate this feast, joy - ful be - yond mea - sure.

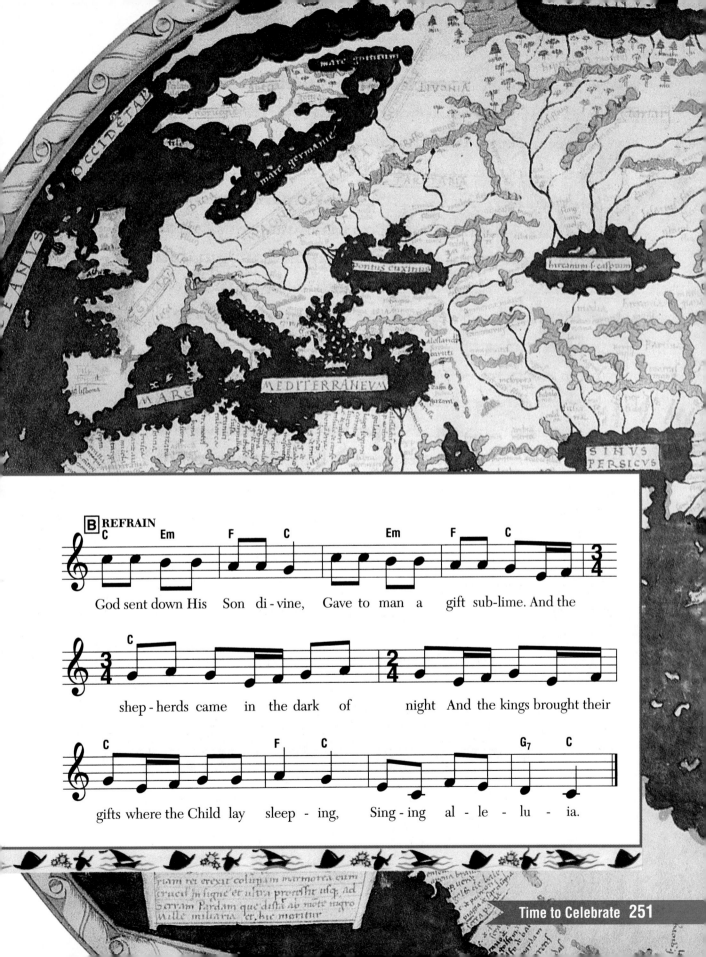

B REFRAIN

God sent down His Son di-vine, Gave to man a gift sub-lime. And the
shep-herds came in the dark of night And the kings brought their
gifts where the Child lay sleep - ing, Sing - ing al - le - lu - ia.

THREE KING'S DAY

In Puerto Rico, Christmas is celebrated for many days, beginning on Christmas Eve and continuing until Three King's Day, on the sixth of January.

The Kings from the East *(Los reyes de Oriente)*

English Words by Aura Kontra   Aguinaldo from Puerto Rico

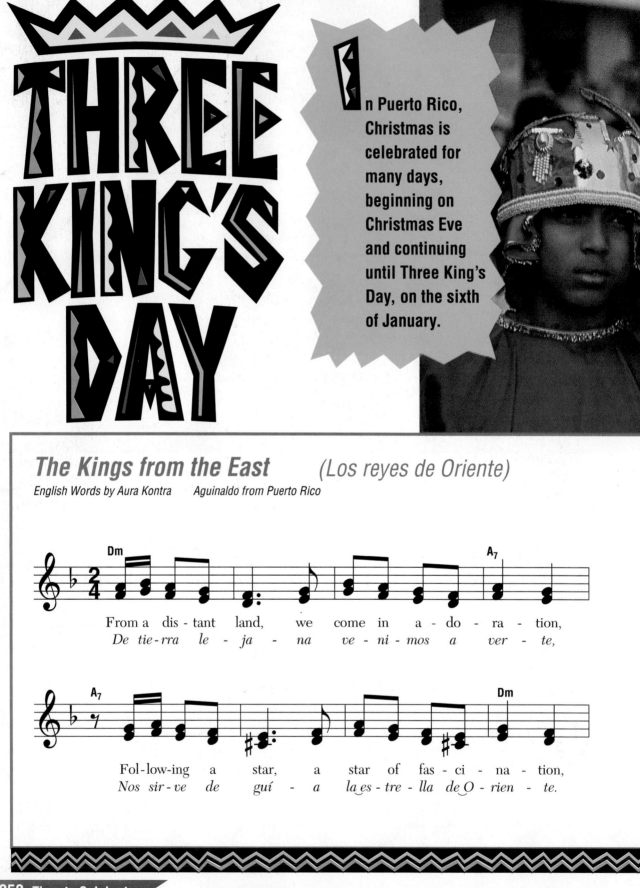

From a dis - tant land,   we   come in   a - do - ra - tion,
De tie - rra le - ja - na ve - ni - mos a ver - te,

Fol - low - ing   a   star,   a   star of fas - ci - na - tion,
Nos sir - ve de   guí - a   la es - tre - lla de O - rien - te.

Shin-ing star so bright, till dawn you rule the night, ___
¡Oh, bri - llan - te_es - tre - lla que_a-nun - cias la_au - ro - ra,

Nev-er cease to guide us with your kind - ly light. _____
No me fal - te nun - ca tu luz bien-he - cho - ra! ___

A CHRISTMAS SPIRITUAL

Join in on the chorus parts of this
spiritual that is sung in solo-chorus style.

Rise Up, Shepherd, and Follow

African American Spiritual

Solo
1. There's a star in the East on Christ - mas morn,
2. If you take good heed of the an - gel's words,

Chorus
Rise up, shep - herd, and fol - low.

Solo
It will lead to the place where the babe is born,
You'll for - get your flocks, you'll for - get your herds,

Menotti wrote his opera *Amahl and the Night Visitors* for television.
The first performance was on Christmas Eve, 1951.

"Shepherd's Dance" from *Amahl and
the Night Visitors* ....Gian Carlo Menotti

Chorus

Rise up, shep - herd, and fol - low.

REFRAIN

Fol - low, fol - low, Rise up, shep - herd, and

fol - low. Fol - low the star of Beth - le - hem, _____

Rise up, shep - herd, and fol - low.

IN THE NEW YEAR

In many parts of the world, chiming bells signal important events. In Japan, temple bells toll 108 times on New Year's Eve. Hitotsu-toya means "counting song" and refers to the counting of the bell sounds. Kasuga Yama is Japanese for Kasuga Mountain. Battledore is the paddle used in a game similar to badminton.

Hitotsu-toya

Folk Song from Japan   *Arranged by Patricia Shehan Campbell*

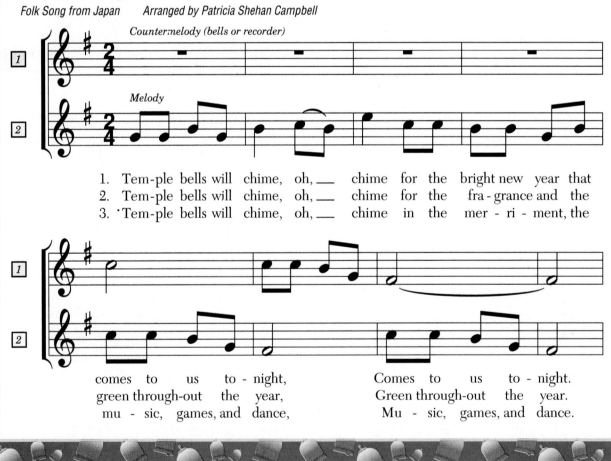

1. Tem-ple bells will chime, oh, ___ chime for the bright new year that
2. Tem-ple bells will chime, oh, ___ chime for the fra-grance and the
3. Tem-ple bells will chime, oh, ___ chime in the mer-ri-ment, the

comes to us to-night,   Comes to us to-night.
green through-out the year,   Green through-out the year.
mu-sic, games, and dance,   Mu-sic, games, and dance.

Now on ev - 'ry door there hangs a spray of love-ly pine, a -
Of the fine and health-y pine on Ka - su - ga Ya - ma, on ___
Peo-ple swing the bat-tle-dore. This is the time to play. This ___

spray of love - ly pine.
Ka - su - ga Ya - ma.
is the day to play.

Hats Off To

This old Scottish song is sung as an expression of friendship.
It is often sung to welcome the new year.

Auld Lang Syne

Poem by Robert Burns — *Traditional Tune from Scotland*

1. Should auld ac-quaint-ance be for-got, And nev-er brought to mind?
2. And here's a hand, my trust-y friend, And give us a hand of thine,

Should auld ac-quaint-ance be for-got, And days of auld lang syne?
We'll take a cup of kind-ness yet, For auld__ lang__ syne.

FRIENDSHIP!

REFRAIN

For auld __ lang __ syne, my dear, For auld __ lang __ syne,

We'll take a cup of kind-ness yet, For auld __ lang __ syne.

SHH!
We're Writing The Constitution

by
Carmino Ravosa

Suggested by the book SHH! WE'RE WRITING THE
CONSTITUTION by Jean Fritz, © 1987 by Jean Fritz.

The Thing That Holds Us Together

Words and Music by Carmino Ravosa

We've Got to Be One People

Words and Music by Carmino Ravosa

We've got to be one peo-ple, we've got to be one coun-try, We've got to be one na-tion if we are to sur-vive. We've got to be one peo-ple, we've got to be one coun-try, We've got to be one na-tion if we are to sur-vive.

1. We've got to stop this act-ing in-de-pen-dent. It's time for us to act and feel as one. We've
2. I've got to say it clear, it's now or nev-er. We can't let this mo-ment get a-way. We've

we are to sur-vive.

Critical Moment

Words and Music by Carmino Ravosa

Shh! We're Writing the Constitution

Words and Music by Carmino Ravosa

REFRAIN
Chorus

Shh! we're writ-ing the Con - sti - tu - tion, shh! we're writ-ing the

Last time to Coda

Con-sti - tu-tion, shh! we're writ-ing the Con-sti - tu-tion, Shh!

1. ↱
2. We
3. ↱
4. We

VERSE

We will do it, we will try it, if we get some peace and qui - et.
can't be bril-liant, can't be wise, and get bit - ten by these flies.
It's as hot as it can get. All we do is sit and sweat.
must keep se - cret what we do, Not a word must come from you or

The Give and Take

Words and Music by Carmino Ravosa

The Best That We Could Do

Words and Music by Carmino Ravosa

where the sol - u - tion lies! It's the

Coda

give and take that make a bar - gain go! ____ Go!

Solo 1; Chorus on repeats

It's the best that we could do. Now the rest is up to you, A -

mer - i - ca. A - mer - i - ca. It's the best that we could make, It's the

3rd time to Coda

test for you to take, A - mer - i - ca. A - mer - i - ca. Solo 2

1. We
2.

know it's not per - fect, well, nei - ther am I. So it's not per - fect, Let's
Some parts are right ____ and some may be wrong. But we can change it ____ as

Chorus

give it a try. (give it a try) It's the
time goes a - long. (time goes a - long) It's the

Coda

mer - i - ca, A - mer - i - ca, A - mer - i - ca. ____

READING

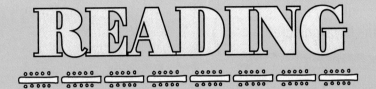

You know how to read the lyrics of a song,
but can you read the notes?

Can you sight-read the
instrumental parts in your book?

You will be able to do so through
the READING connection.

By using solfa and rhythm syllables,
you will learn to read music in various modes
and meters as well as music made up of
many different rhythm patterns.

Before long you will be able to look at a
song and know how it will sound—
even before you sing it!

You will have made
the READING connection.

A Pentatonic Song

Can you figure out why there is no B♭ sign in the key signature?

Buffalo Boy

Folk Song from the United States Adapted by Jean Sinor

1. When are we gon-na get mar - ried, mar - ried, mar - ried?
   When are we gon-na get mar - ried, Dear old buf-fa-lo boy?

2. I guess we'll marry in a week, a week, a week.
   I guess we'll marry in a week, that is if the weather be good.

3. How're you gonna come to the wedding, the wedding, the wedding?
   How're you gonna come to the wedding, Dear old buffalo boy?

4. I guess I'll come in my ox cart, ox cart, ox cart.
   I guess I'll come in my ox cart, that is if the weather be good.

5. There ain't gonna be a wedding, a wedding, a wedding.
   There ain't gonna be a wedding, not even if the weather be good.

$\frac{2}{4}$ METER ☙ $\frac{4}{4}$ METER

Feel the difference between $\frac{4}{4}$ meter and $\frac{2}{4}$ meter as you sing these songs.

Ballad of the Boll Weevil

Folk Song from Southern United States   *Adapted by Jean Sinor*

1. The boll wee-vil was a lit-tle black bug from

Mex - i - co, they say, Come all the way to

Tex - as, Just to find a place to stay.

Refrain   Just a-lookin' for a home, . . . *(4 times)*

2. The first time I saw the boll weevil,
   he was standing on the square,
   The next time I saw the boll weevil,
   he had his whole family there. *Refrain*

3. The farmer took the boll weevil
   and put him in the sand,
   The weevil said to the farmer,
   "I can stand it like a man." *Refrain*

Weevily Wheat

Traditional

Don't want your weev-i-ly wheat, Don't want your bar - ley.

Take some flour in half an hour and bake a cake for Char - lie.

A Hexachordal Song

Look through the song and identify all the pitches used.
Can you figure out what *hexachordal* means?

Nobody's Business

Play-Party Game Song

1. I went to town in a lit-tle red wa-gon,
2. I've got a wife and she's a dai-sy,

Came back home with the hub a-drag-gin'.
She won't work and I'm too la-zy.

It's no-bod-y's bus-'ness what I do.
It's no-bod-y's bus-'ness what I do.

REFRAIN

It's no-bod-y's bus-'ness, bus-'ness, No-bod-y's bus-'ness, bus-'ness,

No-bod-y's bus-'ness what I do.

From PLAY-PARTY GAMES. World Around Songs.

Conducting the Meter

What conducting pattern will you use for this song?

A Canadian Lad

Folk Song from Canada

1. Once a Ca - na - dian lad, Ex - iled from hearth and home,
2. "If you should reach my land, My most un - hap - py land,
3. "My own be - lov - ed land I'll not for - get till death,

Wan - dered, a - lone and sad, Through a - lien lands un - known.
Please speak to all my friends So they will un - der - stand.
And I will speak of her With my last dy - ing breath.

Down by a rush - ing stream, Thought-ful and sad one day,
Tell them how much I wish That I could be once more
My own be - lov - ed land I'll not for - get till death,

He watched the riv - er flow, And to it he did say:
In my be - lov - ed land That I will see no more.
And I will speak of her With my last dy - ing breath."

it all together by combining "Leila" and
he Clap-and-Tap pattern.

Leila

Folk Song from North Carolina

Lei - la, that's shoo my love, Lei - la, that's shoo my love,

Turn me in a hur - ry now. Shoo Dol - ly, shoo my love,

Turn me in a hur - ry now. Shoo Dol - ly, shoo my love.

Clap and Tap

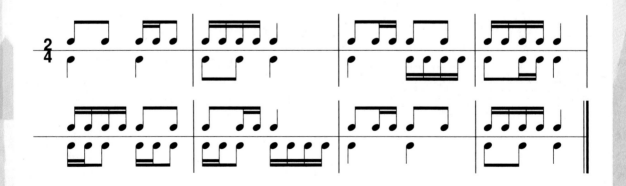

All About Hexachords

Find the notes of these hexachordal scales on the keyboard below.

If *C* is *do:*

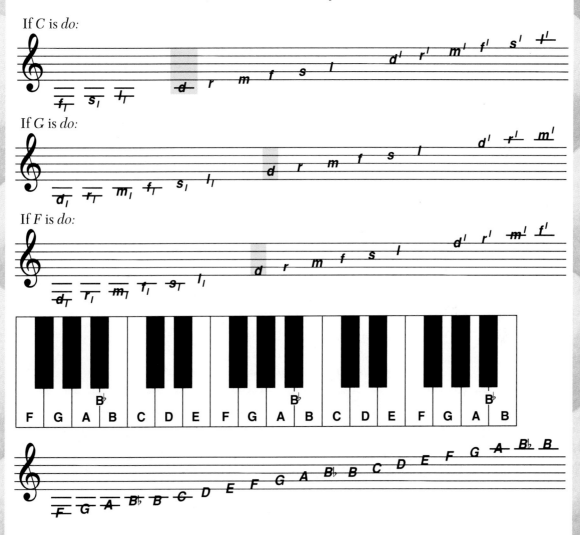

If *G* is *do:*

If *F* is *do:*

Follow the Map

Here is a very simple song written in a very tricky way. Can you figure it out?

Close Your Eyes (Fais Dodo)

Folk Song from France   Adapted by Jean Sinor

Close your eyes and sleep now my broth - er,
Close your eyes, you'll   have a sur - prise.

Your fath - er will brew hot choco-late for you,
Your moth - er will bake a won - der - ful cake.

Fais dodo, 'Co-las, mon p'tit frére
Fais dodo, T'au ras du lo lo.
Papa est en bas, il fait du choc'lat,
Maman est en haut, elle fait du gateau.
Fais dodo, 'Co-las, mon p'tit frére
Fais dodo, T'au ras du lo lo.

Here is a countermelody for the song. Notice where the two voices sing the same note. This is called *unison*.

A Lullaby From Wales

Can you analyze the phrase form of this song?

All Through the Night

Verse 1 by Harold Boulton   *Melody from Wales*

Sleep, my child, and peace at-tend thee, All through the night;

Guard - ian an - gels God will send thee, All through the night.

Soft the drow - sy hours are creep-ing, Hill and vale in slum - ber steep-ing,

I my lov - ing vig - il keep - ing, All through the night.

An Unhappy Tale

Try playing the last phrase of this ballad on a recorder.

Wagoner's Lad

Folk Song from the United States   *As Collected by Jean Sinor*

1. I am ___ a poor girl whose ___ for - tune is bad,

Who's a long time been court - ed by the wa - gon - er's lad.

He court - ed me du - ly by night and by day,

and ___ now he is packed ___ and is go - ing a - way.

2. "Your horses are hungry, go feed them some hay,
   and set you down by me as long as you stay."
   "My horses ain't hungry, they won't eat your hay.
   So fare you well, Nancy, I've no time to stay."

3. So early next morning as he did arise,
   He crossed the deep waters with tears in his eyes,
   To think he must leave her and see her no more.
   He left this girl weeping on New River's shore.

Tricky Rhythms

Do you recognize this song? Sing it with the rhythm accompaniment.

A Rhythm Canon

Two Canons About Bells

Do the notes in the color boxes move up or down?

The Little Bells of Westminster

Traditional Round

The lit-tle bells of West-min-ster go ding, dong, ding, dong, dong.

Evening Stars

English Words by Jean Sinor   *Folk Song from Hungary*   *Collected by Jean Sinor*

Eve - ning stars be - gin to glow,

Eve - ning bells are soft and low, Bim bam bom,

Bim bam bom, Eve - ning bells are soft and low.

Here is a song that partners with itself.

Zum Gali Gali

Folk Song from Israel

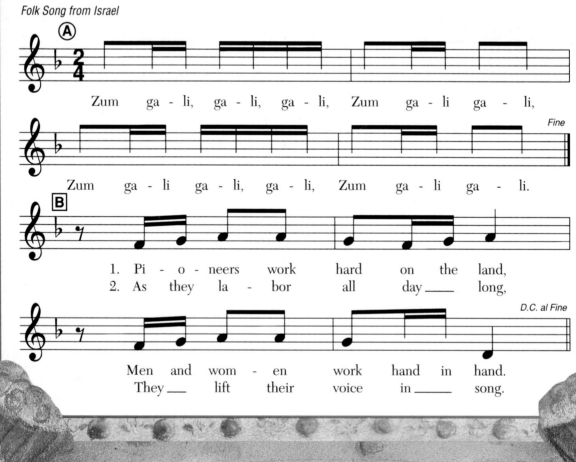

A

Zum ga - li, ga - li, ga - li, Zum ga - li ga - li,

Fine

Zum ga - li ga - li, ga - li, Zum ga - li ga - li.

B

1. Pi - o - neers work hard on the land,
2. As they la - bor all day___ long,

D.C. al Fine

Men and wom - en work hand in hand.
They ___ lift their voice in ___ song.

A COMMON TONIC

Both of these melodies have *la* as the tonic or home tone.

Ay-lye, lyu-lye

English Words by Richard Morris   *Yiddish Folk Song*

1. Ay - lye, lyu - lye, lyu - lye, Go to sleep now, don't cry;

Close your eyes in slum - ber, Oh, my dar - ling kind' - lach.

2. Very soon I'll wake you,
To the fair I'll take you;
There'll be joy and laughter,
Oh, my darling kind'lach.

3. You will find such treats there,
Such good things to eat there;
Rolls with apple butter,
Oh, my darling kind'lach.

4. Ay-lye, lyu-lye, lyu-lye,
Go to sleep now, don't cry;
Close your eyes in slumber,
Oh, my darling kind'lach.

Do the notes in the color boxes sound the same as the notes in the color box in "Ay-lye, lyu-lye"?

l_l d   d   r   d   d

SOMETHING NEW

For Health and Strength

Traditional Round from England

For health and strength and dai - ly food, We praise Thy name, O Lord.

Can you describe where the question mark note is?

For the Beauty of the Earth

Words by Folliot S. Pierpoint   Music by Conrad Kocher

For the beau-ty of the earth, For the beau-ty of the skies,

For the love which from our birth, O-ver and a-round us lies.

REFRAIN

Lord of all, to Thee we raise, This our hymn of grate-ful praise.

A FRENCH FAVORITE

Enjoy singing this song with both the English and French words.

In the Moonlight   (Au clair de la lune)

English Version by D. Auberge   Traditional Song from France

Stand-ing   in   the   moon-light,   Mon   a - mi   Pier - rot,
Au   clair   de   la   lu - ne,   Mon   a - mi   Pier - rot,

I   have   lost   my   can - dle,   How,   I   do   not   know!
Prê - te - moi   ta   plu - me,   Pour   é - crire   un   mot;

If   you   can - not   help   me,   I   will   have   to   stay
Ma   chan - delle   est   mor - te   je   n'ai   plus   de   feu.

Stand-ing   in   the   dark - ness,   'til   the   light   of   day.
Ou - vre - moi   ta   por - te,   Pour   l'a - mour   de   Dieu.

Finding Ti

In what two syllables do you find `ti` on the letter ladder?

Betty Martin

Song from the United States

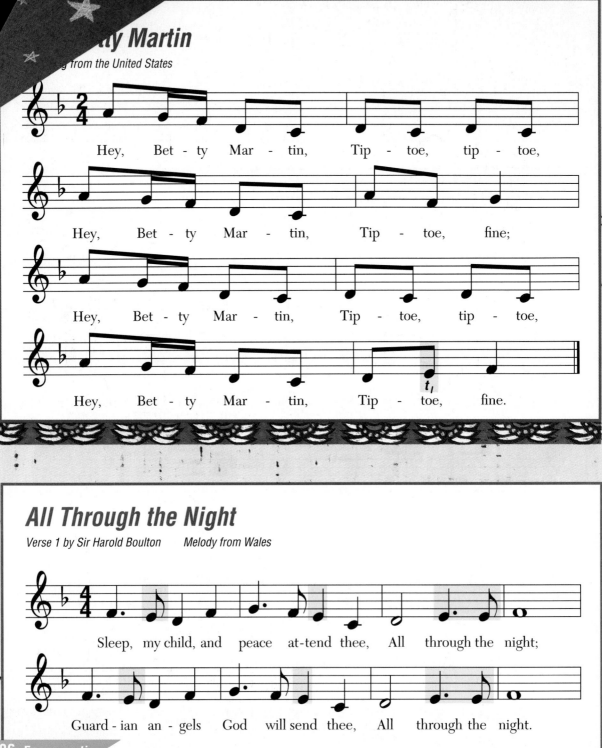

Hey, Bet-ty Mar-tin, Tip-toe, tip-toe,

Hey, Bet-ty Mar-tin, Tip-toe, fine;

Hey, Bet-ty Mar-tin, Tip-toe, tip-toe,

Hey, Bet-ty Mar-tin, Tip-toe, fine.

All Through the Night

Verse 1 by Sir Harold Boulton   *Melody from Wales*

Sleep, my child, and peace at-tend thee, All through the night;

Guard-ian an-gels God will send thee, All through the night.

Soft the drow-sy hours are creep-ing, Hill and vale in slum-ber steep-ing,

I my lov-ing vig-il keep-ing, All through the night.

The Roland P. Murdock Collection, Wichita Art Museum, Wichita, Kansas.

Mother and Child   *Mary Cassatt*

Can you find two phrases that are the same?

The Huron Carol

English Words by J. E. Middleton   *Christmas Carol from Canada*

'Twas in the moon of win-ter-time When all the birds had fled,

That might-y Git-chi Man-i-tou Sent an-gel choirs in-stead.

Be-fore their light the stars grew dim And won-d'ring hunt-ers heard the hymn: —

"Je-sus, your King is born. Je-sus is born. *In ex-cel-sis glo-ri-a!*"

KEY SIGNATURES

If F# is in the key signature, where is *do*?

In the Bleak Midwinter

Words by Christine Rossetti   Music by Gustav Holst

1. In the bleak mid - win - ter, frost - y wind made moan,
Earth stood hard as i - ron, wa - ter like a stone.
Snow had fal - len, snow on snow, snow __ on __ snow,
In the bleak mid - win - ter, long __ a - go.

2. What can I give him, poor as I am?
   If I were a shepherd, I would give a lamb.
   If I were a wise man, I would do my part.
   What I have I give him, give my heart.

HEBREW SONG

Hava Nashira

Round from Israel

The Hebrew words mean "Let us sing a song, a song of alleluia."

I

d s l s d f m r d r d
Ha - va na - shi - ra, Shir al - le - lu - ia!

II

d′ t d′ r′ m′ d′ d′ r′ m′ f′ m′
Ha - va na - shi - ra, Shir al - le - lu - ia!

III

m′ r′ d′ t d′ l s d′ d′ t l t d′
Ha - va na - shi - ra, Shir al - le - lu - ia!

G is My Key

Do these songs end on the tonic?

Viva la musica

Words and Music by Michael Praetorius

I

Vi - va, vi - va la mu - si - ca!

II

Vi - va, vi - va la mu - si - ca!

III

Vi - va la mu - si - ca.

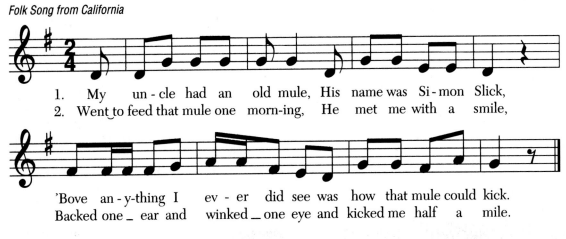

The Kicking Mule

Folk Song from California

1. My un - cle had an old mule, His name was Si - mon Slick,
2. Went to feed that mule one morn-ing, He met me with a smile,

'Bove an - y - thing I ev - er did see was how that mule could kick.
Backed one ear and winked one eye and kicked me half a mile.

Everyone join in on the refrain of this fun folk song.

Doktor Eisenbart

Folk Song of the Pennsylvania Dutch

VERSE

1., 2. I am Herr Dok-tor Ei-sen-bart,
I'll cure your ills with heal-ing art, Twil-li wil-li witt, boom boom!

My pa - tients nev - er can com - plain,
My pa - tients call me "Ir - on Beard,"

Twil - li wil - li witt, boom boom boom boom! They leave with - out an
For all my cures I

ache or pain,
am re - vered,
Twil - li wil - li witt, boom boom!

REFRAIN

Sing to - ri - ay, sing to - ri - ay! Twil - li wil - li witt, boom

boom boom boom! Sing to - ri - ay, sing to - ri - ay!

Twil - li wil - li witt, boom boom

GOODBYE FROM AFRICA

Add percussion parts for a special performance of this song.

Kokoleoko

Folk Song from Liberia

1. Ko - ko - le - o - ko, Ma - ma, Ko - ko - le - o - ko,
2. A - by,* Sa - rah, a - by,
3. One __ more __ round, Te - te, one __ more __ round,
4. Take __ your __ time, chick - en, take __ your __ time,

Ko - ko - le - o - ko, chick - en, crow - ing for day.
A - by, chick - en, crow - ing for day.
One __ more __ round, chick - en, crow - ing for day.
Take __ your __ time, chick - en, crow - ing for day.

Aby means "good-bye"

Shaker played with back and forth movement

Claves

Medium drum played with fingers

Large drum played with heel of hand

TWO MELODIES—
ONE SONG

There are two different melodies in this song.
Keep an eye on the color box to follow your part.

Roll on the Ground, Boys

Folk Song from Mississippi   *Countermelody by Jean Sinor*

Countermelody
Roll, boys, roll-in' all a-round roll - in' on the ground, roll - in' on the ground,

Melody
Roll on the ground, boys, roll on the ground.

Roll, boys, roll-in' all a-round, roll - in' on the ground.

Roll on the ground, boys, roll on the ground.

Roll, boys, roll-in' all a-round; roll - in' on the ground.

String Quartet No. 2, Movement 3 (excerpt)
..............Franz Joseph Haydn

Add a Countermelody

Learn to sing both melodies of this lullaby.

All the Pretty Little Horses

Folk Song from Southern United States

1 Countermelody

Hush - a - bye, sleep-y ba - by,

2 Melody

Hush-a - bye, don't you cry, Go to sleep-y, lit-tle ba - by.

1

You _____ will have six white hors - es,

2

When you wake, you will have all the pret-ty lit-tle hors - es:

Original melody collected, adapted, and arranged by John A. and Alan Lomax. TRO–© Copyright 1934 (renewed)
Ludlow Music, Inc., New York, N.Y. Used by permission.

Blacks and bays, _____ six lit-tle hors - es,

Blacks and bays, dap-ples and grays, Coach and six-a lit-tle hors - es.

Hush - a - bye, you sleep - y ba - by.

Hush-a- bye, don't you cry, Go to sleep-y, lit-tle ba - by.

FOUR-PART

Use parts of these songs as recorder ostinatos and add them to a performance.

Old Abram Brown

Words by Walter de la Mare *Music by Benjamin Britten*

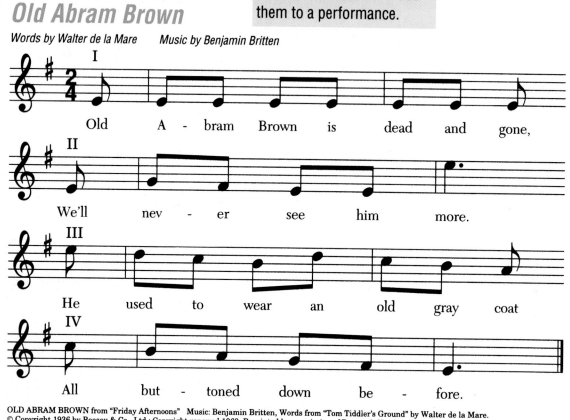

I
Old A - bram Brown is dead and gone,

II
We'll nev - er see him more.

III
He used to wear an old gray coat

IV
All but - toned down be - fore.

OLD ABRAM BROWN from "Friday Afternoons" Music: Benjamin Britten, Words from "Tom Tiddler's Ground" by Walter de la Mare.
© Copyright 1936 by Boosey & Co., Ltd.; Copyright renewed 1963. Reprinted by permission of Boosey & Hawkes, Inc.

ROUNDS

My Dame Hath a Lame, Tame Crane

Traditional Round

I
My dame hath a lame, tame crane,

II
My dame hath a crane that is lame,

III
Pray, gen - tle Jane, let my dame's lame, tame crane

IV
Feed and come home a - gain.

Whether the weather be cold,
Or whether the weather be hot
We'll weather the weather
Whatever the weather,
Whether we like it or not.

Can you make up other
tongue twisters?

MAJOR OR MINOR?

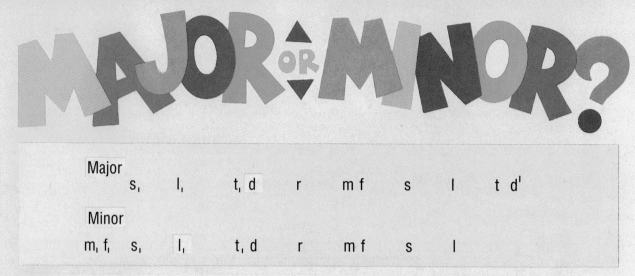

Major

s, l, t, d r mf s l t d'

Minor

m, f, s, l, t, d r mf s l

Sing these songs to decide if they sound major (ending on *do*) or minor (ending on *la*).

All Through the Night

In the Bleak Midwinter

The Huron Carol

Doktor Eisenbart

Old Abram Brown

My Dame Hath a Lame Tame Crane

Hava Nashira

All the Pretty Little Horses

Change the Tonality

Can you sing these songs in a minor tonality? What syllables will you use?

Honey, You Can't Love One

Folk Song from the United States

1. Hon-ey, you can't love one, Hon-ey, you can't love one,
2. Hon-ey, you can't love two, Hon-ey, you can't love two,

You can't love one and still have your fun,
You can't love two and al - ways be true,

Oh, hon - ey, you can't love one.
Oh, hon - ey, you can't love two.

Love Somebody

Folk Song from the United States

Love some-bod - y, yes, I do, Love some-bod - y, yes, I do,

Love some-bod - y, yes, I do, Love some-bod-y but I won't tell who!

SIMILAR PATTERNS

What measures are similar to the first measure?
What is the same and what is different?

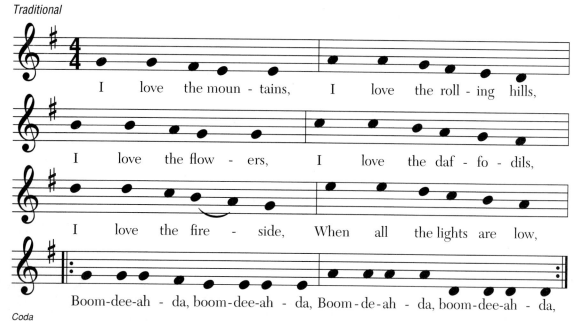

I Love the Mountains

Traditional

I love the moun - tains, I love the roll - ing hills,

I love the flow - ers, I love the daf - fo - dils,

I love the fire - side, When all the lights are low,

Boom-dee-ah - da, boom-dee-ah - da, Boom-de-ah - da, boom-dee-ah - da,

Coda

Boom didledee dum-dum, . . . Boom, boom!

Change the Tonality

Can you sing these songs in a minor tonality? What syllables will you use?

Honey, You Can't Love One

Folk Song from the United States

1. Hon-ey, you can't love one, Hon-ey, you can't love one,
2. Hon-ey, you can't love two, Hon-ey, you can't love two,

You can't love one and still have your fun,
You can't love two and al - ways be true,

Oh, hon - ey, you can't love one.
Oh, hon - ey, you can't love two.

Love Somebody

Folk Song from the United States

Love some-bod - y, yes, I do, Love some-bod - y, yes, I do,

Love some-bod - y, yes, I do, Love some-bod-y but I won't tell who!

MELODIC SEQUENCES

Oleana

English Words by Polly Budd *Emigrant Song from Norway*

Find the melodic sequences in this song about Norwegian emigrants.

1. O - le-an - a, O - le - an - a, Far a-cross the deep blue sea,
O - le - an - a, O - le - an - a, That is where I'd like to be.

REFRAIN: Ole, Oleana, Ole, Oleana,
Ole, Ole, Ole, Ole, Ole, Oleana.

2. Oleana, that's the place,
That is where I'll settle down;
It's a place where land is free
And money trees grow all around. *Refrain*

3. Corn and wheat grow to the sky,
All according to the plan;
Sheep and cows do all the work
And fish jump in the frying pan. *Refrain*

4. There the crops just plant themselves,
There the sun shines night and day;
Harvest time comes once a month,
But farmers only sing and play. *Refrain*

5. Ole Bull will play for us,
Play upon his violin;
And we'll sing and dance together,
Happier than we've ever been. *Refrain*

Sing sequences to these motives.

s   l

d   r

s   l

d¹   t

A Play Party Song

The words will tell you how to dance this play-party song.

Shake Them 'Simmons Down

Folk Song from the United States

1. Cir - cle right,   do - oh, do - oh, Cir - cle right,   do - oh, do - oh,

Cir - cle right,   do - oh, do - oh, Shake them 'sim-mons   down.

2. Circle left, . . .
3. Girls to the center, . . .
4. Boys to the center, . . .

5. Balance all, . . .
6. Promenade, . . .

Sing this version of these songs, then sing them the way they are
supposed to be.

I   love   the   moun - tains,   I   love   the   roll - ing   hills, . . .

Ly - de - o,   ly - de - o,   da - day,   Ly - de - o,   ly - de - ay - de

Shoo, fly,   don't both - er   me,   shoo, fly,   don't both - er   me,

DOTTED NOTES

Can you feel the difference between even and uneven (dotted) patterns?

Shoo, Fly
Game Song from the United States

Shoo, fly, don't both - er me, Shoo, fly, don't both - er me,

Shoo, fly, don't both - er me, For I be-long to some-bod - y.

I feel, I feel, I feel, I feel like a morn-ing star,

I feel, I feel, I feel, I feel, I feel like a morn-ing star. So,

Sandy Land
Folk Song from Oklahoma

Make my liv-in' in sand - y land, Make my liv-in' in sand - y land,

Make my liv-in' in sand - y land, La - dies, fare - you - well.

This humorous song was one of the hand-clapping, toe-tapping tunes that added to the fun at barn dances in the pioneer days of America.

Old Joe Clark

Words by Raymond Matthews   *Folk Song from the United States*

1. Old Joe Clark, he built a house,
   Took him 'bout a week;
   He built the floors above his head,
   The ceilings under his feet.

   REFRAIN
   Rock-a-rock, Old Joe Clark,
   Rock-a-rock, I'm gone;
   Rock-a-rock, Old Joe Clark,
   Good-bye, Lucy Long.

2. Old Joe Clark, he had a dog,
   Like none you've ever seen;
   With floppy ears and a curly tail,
   And six feet in between. *Refrain*

3. Old Joe Clark, he had a wife,
   Her name was Betty Sue;
   She had two great big brown eyes,
   The other two were blue. *Refrain*

4. I went down to Old Joe's house,
   Never been there before,
   He slept on the feather bed,
   I slept on the floor. *Refrain*

5. Joe Clark had a violin,
   He fiddled all the day,
   Anybody start to dance.
   And Joe would start to play. *Refrain*

Listen to the short-long
patterns in this song.

We're Going Round the Mountain

Folk Song from Mississippi

1. We're go - ing round the moun - tain, two by two,

We're go - ing round the moun - tain, two by two,

We're go - ing round the moun - tain, two by two,

So rise, Sal - ly, rise.

2. Let me see you make a
   motion, two by two, . . .

3. That's a mighty poor
   motion, two by two, . . .

Clap this rhythm pattern, using the rhythm of the word *Sally* along
with the usual syllables.

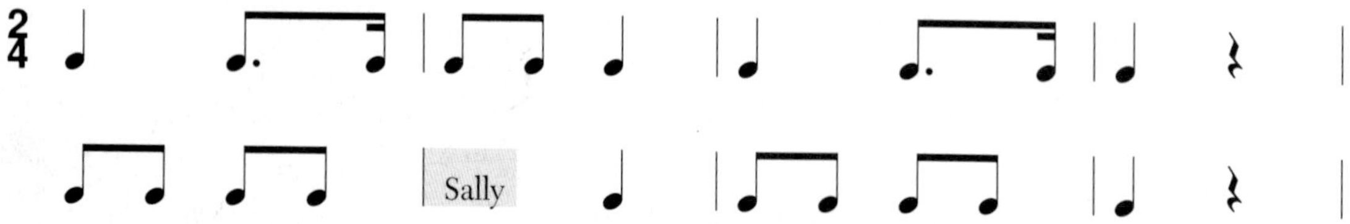

Sally

A MUSICAL SIGN

Do you know what *Dal segno al Fine* means?

Hoosen Johnny

Folk Song from Illinois

1. The lit-tle black bull came down the mead-ow, Hoo-sen John-ny, Hoo-sen John-ny,

Fine

The lit-tle black bull came down the mead-ow, Long time a - go.

Dal segno al Fine

Long time a - go, Long time a - go.

2. First he pawed and then he bellowed, . . .

SING WITH JOY!

Can you sing this song with rhythm syllables? Find the measures that are upbeats.

Going to Church
Wm. H. Johnson,

National Museum of American Art, Washington D.C.

Get on Board

African American Spiritual

REFRAIN

Get on   board,   lit-tle chil-dren, Get on   board,   lit-tle chil-dren,

Fine

Get on   board,   lit-tle chil-dren,   There's room for man-y - a - more.

VERSE

The   gos-pel train's a - com-ing,   I   hear it close at   hand, _____

Da Capo al Fine

I   hear the car-wheels rum-bling And   roll-ing through the   land.

VOICES FROM KOREA

As you listen to this song, pay close attention to the rhythm pattern in the color box.

Arirang

English Words by Alice Firgau   *Folk Song from Korea*

A - ri - rang, A - ri - rang, a - ra - ri - yo,
A - ri - rang, A - ri - rang, a - ra - ri - yo,

A - ri - rang ko - ge - ro nuh - muh - kan - da.
O - ver the hills of A - ri - rang.

Chung - chun ha - nul - en pyul - do man - ko,
Voic - es call me from far a - way,

I neh ka - sem - en su - sim - do man - ta
I must fol - low, I can - not stay.

Rippling Water

Can you find similarities between this song and the song on page 311?

Waters Ripple and Flow

English Words by Marta Novak   *Folk Song from Slovakia*

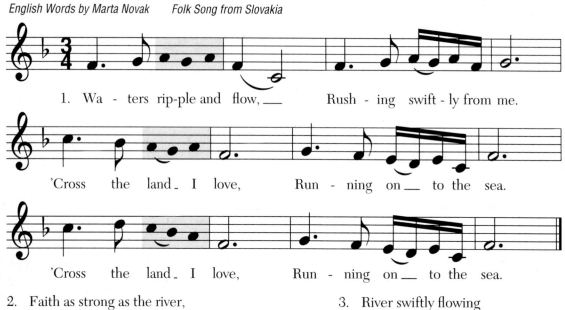

1. Wa - ters rip-ple and flow, ___ Rush - ing swift - ly from me.

'Cross the land _ I love, Run - ning on ___ to the sea.

'Cross the land _ I love, Run - ning on ___ to the sea.

2. Faith as strong as the river,
   Courage wide as the sea.
   For the land I love,
   For the right to be free. } *(2 times)*

3. River swiftly flowing
   Heed my yearning heart.
   Someday I will return,
   Never to depart. } *(2 times)*

THREE NOTE PATTERNS

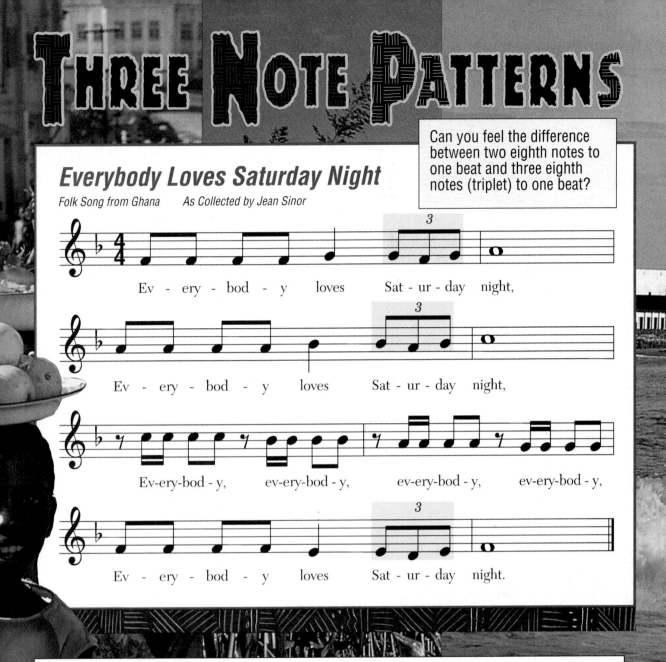

Everybody Loves Saturday Night

Folk Song from Ghana   *As Collected by Jean Sinor*

Ev - ery - bod - y loves Sat - ur - day night,

Ev - ery - bod - y loves Sat - ur - day night,

Ev-ery-bod - y, ev-ery-bod - y, ev-ery-bod - y, ev-ery-bod - y,

Ev - ery - bod - y loves Sat - ur - day night.

Can you feel the difference between two eighth notes to one beat and three eighth notes (triplet) to one beat?

Rhythm Canon

Read this canon, first with rhythm syllables in unison, and then clap
it as a two-part canon.

Which Part Will You Play?

Do you want to be Oliver, the old woman, or the tree?
Act out the story of this old English song.

Oliver Cromwell

Folk Song from England

1. Oliver Cromwell lies buried and dead,
Hee-haw, buried and dead.
They planted an apple tree over his head,
Hee-haw, over his head.

2. The apples were ripe and ready to fall,
Hee-haw, ready to fall.
There came an old woman to gather them all,
Hee-haw, gather them all.

3. Oliver rose and gave her a drop,
Hee-haw, gave her a drop,
Which made the old woman go hippity-hop,
Hee-haw, hippity-hop.

After the Battle of Naseby, 1645. *Sir John Gilbert.*

Watercolor, painted 1860 Towneley Hall Art Gallery & Museum, Burnley, England.

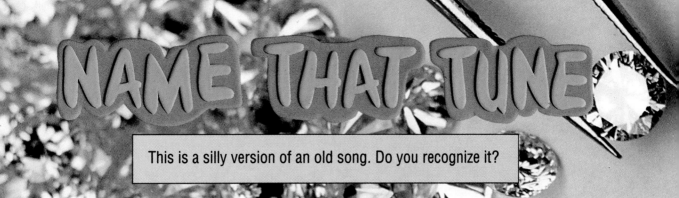

NAME THAT TUNE

This is a silly version of an old song. Do you recognize it?

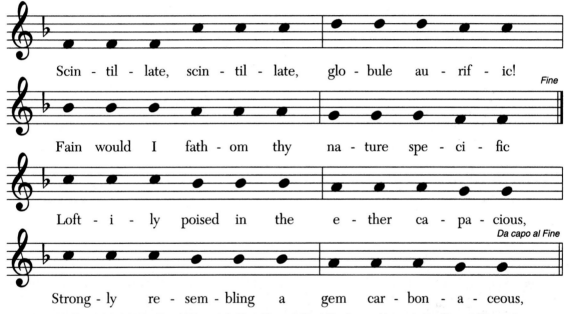

Scintillate, Scintillate

Anonymous Parody

Scin - til - late, scin - til - late, glo - bule au - rif - ic!

Fine

Fain would I fath - om thy na - ture spe - ci - fic

Loft - i - ly poised in the e - ther ca - pa - cious,

Da capo al Fine

Strong - ly re - sem - bling a gem car - bon - a - ceous,

From THE FIRESIDE BOOK OF FUN AND GAMES © 1974 by Marie Winn and Allan Miller. Reprinted by permission of Simon & Schuster, Inc.

Here are some definitions to help you out.

aurific—golden

capacious—spacious, large

carbonaceous—of carbon or coal

ether—space

fain—gladly

fathom—understand

gem—precious stone

loftily—up high

scintillate—shine, sparkle

DUPLE METER

Here is a very early canon. It's in a very old-fashioned kind of English. Can you figure out the words?

Sumer is icumen in

Thirteenth-Century Canon from England

I   II

Sum - er is i - cum - en in, _____ Lhu - de sing cu - cu;

Grow - eth sed and blow - eth med, And spring - eth wo - de nu,

Sing cu - cu; Mu - rie sing cu - cu.

Vive la Compagnie

The words below are grouped according to beats.
Point to each group of words on the beat as you sing.

Vive L'Amour

College Song

Let	ev'ry good	fellow now	join in a	song,
	Vive la	com-pa-	gnie!	
Suc-	cess to each	other and	pass it a-	long,
	Vive la	com-pa-	gnie!	
	Vive la	vive la	vive l'a-	mour,
	Vive la	vive la	vive l'a-	mour,
	Vive la	vive la	vive l'a-	mour,
	Vive la	com-pa-	gnie!	

What's the Meter?

As you sing "Oliver Cromwell," feel two beats to a measure.

Oliver Cromwell

Folk Song from England

Ol - i - ver Crom - well lies bur - ied and dead;

Hee - haw, bur - ied and dead.

Here is another song in $\frac{6}{8}$ meter. Do you recognize it?

Stars of the Heavens (Las estrellitas del cielo)

English Words by Aura Kontra   Folk Song from Mexico

Stars of the heav-ens are wink - ing, With sil - v'ry light they are
Las es - tre - lli - tas del cie - lo Bri - llan con su luz de

twin - kling. A heav - en - ly rid - er came jing - ling
pla - ta. ____ San - tia - go las fue sem - bran - do

With sil - v'ry spurs, star - light sprin - kling.
Con sus es - pue - las de pla - ta.

Can you make up new verses for this folk song?

Down Home

Folk Song from Pennsylvania

1. Down home we have an old, old shack,

The bats fly out but sneak right back!

REFRAIN

High lee, high low, high lee, high low,

How we get by I do not know!

2. Down home we have an old, old cow,
   Two golden horns grow out of her brow! . . .

3. Down home we have an old, old bull,
   He eats and eats and never gets full! . . .

4. Down home we have an old, old goose,
   Her neck's a foot long and her feathers are loose! . . .

Reprinted by permission of the American Folklore Society.

DO YOU RECOGNIZE THIS SONG?

Choose a partner and perform this two-part rhythm in $\frac{6}{8}$ meter.

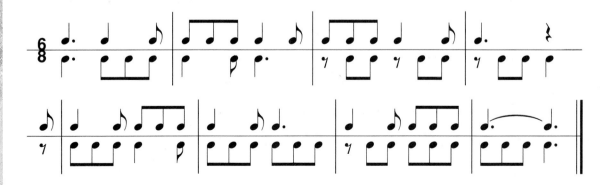

This is a silly version of an old song. Can you tell what one it is?

Three Myopic Rodents

Anonymous Parody

Three myopic rodents, Three myopic rodents.
Observe how they perambulate, Observe how they perambulate.
They all circumnavigated the agriculturalist's spouse.
She excised their extremities with a carving utensil.
Did you ever regard such an occurrence in your existence
As three myopic rodents?

From THE FIRESIDE BOOK OF FUN AND GAMES © 1974 by Marie Winn and Alan Miller.
Reprinted by permission of Simon & Schuster, Inc.

What impossible things are described in this tall tale?

The Derby Ram

Folk Song from the Ozarks

VERSE

1. Oh, as I went down to Der - by town, all on a sum-mer's day, ___
It's there I saw the fin - est ram that's ev - er fed on hay. ___

And if you don't be-lieve __ me And think I tell a lie, ____

Just you go down to Der-by And you'll see the same as I. ____

2. Oh, the wool upon this ram's back,
   It drug to the ground,
   And I hauled it to the market
   And it weighed ten thousand pounds.
   Refrain

3. Oh, the horns upon this ram's head,
   They reached to the moon,
   For the butcher went up on February
   And never got back till June.
   Refrain

4. Oh, the ears upon this ram's head,
   They reached to the sky,
   And the eagle built his nest there
   For I heard the young ones cry.
   Refrain

5. Oh, every tooth this ram had
   Would hold a bushel of corn,
   And every foot he stood on
   Would cover an acre of ground.
   Refrain

WELCOME HOME

Is this song in a major or in a minor key?

When Johnny Comes Marching Home

Words and Music by Patrick S. Gilmore

1. When John-ny comes march-ing home a-gain, Hur - rah! ___ Hur - rah! ___

We'll give him a heart - y wel - come then, Hur - rah! ___ Hur - rah! ___

The _ men will cheer, _ the boys will shout, The la - dies they _ will all turn out,

And we'll shout "Hur - rah" when John-ny comes march-ing home! __

2. Let love and friendship on the day, Hurrah! Hurrah!
   Their choicest treasure then display, Hurrah! Hurrah!
   And let each one perform some part,
   To fill with joy the warrior's heart,
   And we'll shout "Hurrah" when Johnny comes marching home!

3. Get ready for the jubilee, Hurrah! Hurrah!
   We'll give the hero three times three, Hurrah! Hurrah!
   The laurel wreath is ready now
   To place upon his royal brow,
   And we'll shout "Hurrah" when Johnny comes marching home!

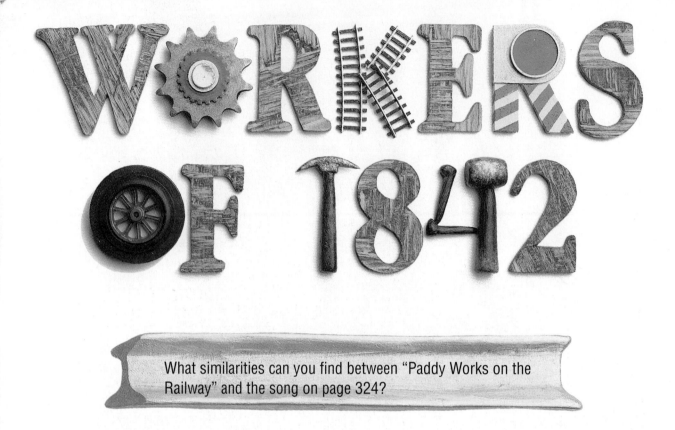

WORKERS OF 1842

What similarities can you find between "Paddy Works on the Railway" and the song on page 324?

Paddy Works on the Railway

Irish American Railroad Song

1. In eight - een hun - dred and for - ty - one, I put my cor - du - roy breech - es on, I put my cor - du - roy breech - es on to work up - on the rail - way.

Chorus
REFRAIN

Fil - li - mee-oo - ree - oo - ree - ay,   Fil - li - mee-oo - ree - oo - ree - ay,

Fil - li - mee-oo - ree - oo - ree - ay,   To work up - on the rail - way.

2. In eighteen hundred and forty-two,
   I left the old world for the new,
   Oh, spare me the luck that brought me
      through
   To work upon the railway.   *Refrain*

3. It's "Pat, do this," and "Pat, do that,"
   Without a stocking or cravat,
   And nothing but an old straw hat,
   While working on the railway.   *Refrain*

Vive L'Amour

College Song

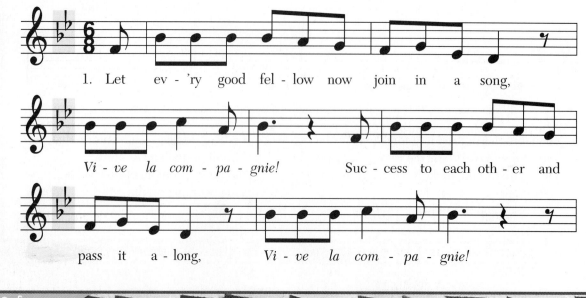

1. Let ev - 'ry good fel - low now join in a song,

Vi - ve la com - pa - gnie! Suc - cess to each oth - er and

pass it a - long, Vi - ve la com - pa - gnie!

Vi - ve la, vi - ve la, vi - ve l'a - mour,

Vi - ve la, vi - ve la, vi - ve l'a - mour,

Vi - ve l'a-mour, Vi - ve l'a-mour, Vi - ve la com - pa - gnie! ___

2. Come all ye good ladies and join in the song, . . .
Sing out with bright voices and help it along, . . .

3. A friend on the left and a friend on the right, . . .
A song of good friendship we're singing tonight, . . .

330 $\frac{6}{8}$ Meter

TERRY KOVALCIK

Do you know how major and minor keys are related?

If C is *do*: C major or A minor

If G is *do*: G major or E minor

If F is *do*: F major or D minor

If D is *do*: D major or B minor

If B♭ is *do*: B♭ major or G minor

Playing the Recorder

Using your left hand, cover the holes shown in the first diagram. Cover the top of the mouthpiece with your lips. Blow gently as you whisper *dahh*. You will be playing G.

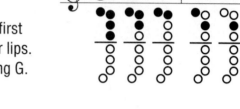

When you can play G, A, and B, you will be able to play phrases 1, 2, and 4 of "In the Moonlight," on page 285.

Practice playing two notes—high C and high D. When you can play them, you are ready to try "Love Somebody," on page 301.

Learn new notes in pairs: D, E and F, C. Cover the holes securely with your fingers and whisper *dahh* as you play in the low register of the recorder. When you can play D and E, try "Shake Them 'Simmons Down," on page 305.

When you can play F and C securely, you are ready to try "Sandy Land," on page 306.

Follow the rule of 1/2 step to play F#, G# (Ab), and Bb.

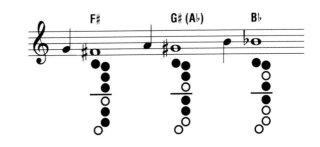

Rule of $\frac{1}{2}$ Step:

To go down one–half step from a given pitch, skip a hole and add two holes.

Play F# in this ostinato for "Little Bells of Westminster," on page 281.

Play G# in this ostinato for "Tumba," on page 62.

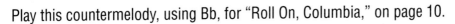

Play this countermelody, using Bb, for "Roll On, Columbia," on page 10.

All the notes needed for recorder ostinatos, melodies, countermelodies, and ensembles are listed in this fingering chart.

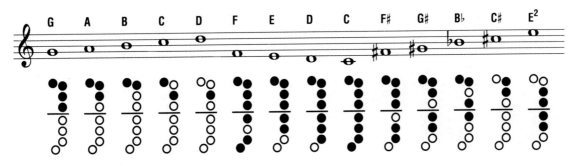

SOUND BANK

ARPA *See* JAROCHO ENSEMBLE.

BASSOON A large, tube-shaped, wooden wind instrument with a double reed and metal keys on the side.

Lower notes on the bassoon may sound gruff and comical. Higher notes are the ones fifth graders sing, and these are softer, sweeter, and gentler. (p. 122)

CELLO (CHEH loh) A large wooden string instrument which may be plucked with the fingers or played with a bow. The player sits with the cello between his or her knees and reaches around the front to play.

The cello has a rich-sounding, warm voice. It can make low notes but can also reach the higher notes fifth graders sing. (p. 122)

CHARANGO (chah RAHN goh) A small guitar that has five double sets of strings. It may have a round back (made either from the shell of an armadillo or from carved wood) or a flat back (made of cedar or walnut). The strings are strummed and/or plucked with the fingernails.

The charango is used in Andean music. It has a sharp, high-pitched sound. (p. 86)

CLARINET A cylinder-shaped wind instrument, usually made of wood. There are holes and metal keys on the side of the clarinet and a reed in the mouthpiece.

Low notes on the clarinet are soft and hollow. The middle notes are open and bright, and the highest notes are piercing. (p. 122)

CYMBALS Two metal plates with hand straps. The player holds one cymbal in each hand and quickly claps them together.

Cymbals make a loud, exciting, metallic crash when struck together. (p. 131)

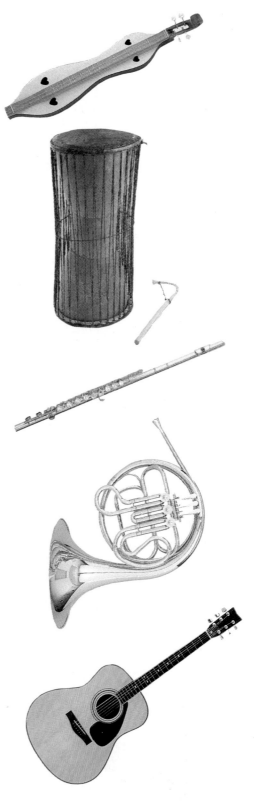

DULCIMER   A soundbox with strings across it. The strings are usually plucked with a quill.

The sound of a dulcimer is quiet and sweet.   (p. 104)

DUNDUN DRUMS   (doon DOON)   West African double-headed drums. Most dundun drums have an hourglass shape. The ends are covered with goatskin drumheads that are fastened together with thongs or cords stretched down the length of the drum. Pressing the cords tightens the drumheads, producing sharp and high sounds.

Dundun drums are known as talking or singing drums because they can match the pitch and rhythm of spoken language.   (p. 182)

FLUTE   A small metal instrument shaped like a pipe, with holes and keys in its side. The player holds the flute sideways and blows across the open mouthpiece.

The sound of the flute is pure and sweet. Its low notes are the ones that fifth graders sing, but it can go much higher. (p. 122)

FRENCH HORN   A medium-sized instrument made of coiled brass tubing. At one end is a large bell and at the other is a funnel-shaped mouthpiece. The player holds the horn on his or her lap and keeps one hand inside the bell. Valves on the side of the horn are pressed to change pitch.

The horn has a mellow, warm tone. Its clearest notes are the same ones fifth graders sing, but the French horn can also go higher and lower.   (p. 122)

GUITAR   A wooden string instrument with six strings. The player strums or plucks the strings with a pick or the fingers to play a melody or chords. Some guitars are electric. Electric guitars are flatter than regular guitars, and they must be plugged into an amplifier.

When played softly, the guitar is gentle and sweet. It sounds lush and powerful when it is played louder. Electric guitars can play much louder than regular guitars. They can also make many special sounds.   (p. 202)

JARANA   *See* JAROCHO ENSEMBLE.

JAROCHO ENSEMBLE   (hah ROH choh)

ARPA   (AR pah) A folk harp that has 34 to 36 nylon strings and spans almost five octaves. It is a diatonic instrument and must be retuned to play in a different key.

The arpa is used especially for the *jarocho* music of Veracruz, Mexico. It is also used in central Mexico, in Venezuela, in the mountains of Ecuador and Peru, and in Paraguay and northern Argentina.   (p. 7)

JARANA   (hah RAH nah)   An eight-string guitar used to strum rhythmic accompaniments in various *son* (sohn), or "folk music," ensembles in Mexico.

It is used especially in the central Gulf Coast area in playing *jarocho* (pertaining to Veracruz) music.   (p. 7)

REQUINTO   (reh KEEN toh)   A small guitar that is used to play fast, highly improvisational melodies. The strings are plucked with a long, thin plastic pick.

Like the jarana, the requinto is used in playing *jarocho* songs in the Veracruz area.   (p. 7)

KOTO   (KOH toh)   A 7- to 17-string zither with movable frets. It is known as the national instrument of Japan. The player sits on the floor, either cross-legged or in a kneeling-sitting position.

Sound is produced when the player plucks the silk strings, using the fingers and thumb of the right hand, with a bamboo, bone, or ivory plectrum. The sound of the koto is a little like that of a harp.   (p. 190)

NATIVE AMERICAN FLUTE A handcrafted wind instrument made from wood, cane, clay, bone, or the hollowed-out stalk of a plant. It may have from three to six finger holes. Some flutes are ornately decorated with notches or paints or with leather pieces and beads hanging from it.

The sound of a Native American flute is similar to that of a recorder. Traditionally a solo instrument used for courtship, reflection, healing, and ceremonial gatherings, it has become popular in ensemble performances.   (p. 192)

OBOE A slender wooden wind instrument with a double reed and metal keys and holes in its side.

In its low voice the oboe can sound mysterious and oriental. These are the notes fifth graders can sing. The oboe can also play higher, thinner, sweeter notes.   (p. 122)

PIANO A large keyboard instrument with 88 keys and many strings on the inside. When the player presses the keys, hammers inside the piano strike the strings to make the sounds.

The piano can play high and low tones. Many notes can be sounded at the same time.   (p. 48)

PIPA (PEE puh)   A Chinese string instrument in the shape of a gourd. It has four strings and is one of the oldest of the Chinese instruments.

The pipa can play music in a quiet mood as well as in a loud "military style."   (p. 106)

RECORDER A simple wind instrument with a "whistle" mouthpiece. The recorder is made of wood or of plastic, and there are eight holes in the side.

Recorders come in many sizes, with the larger ones playing lower notes. All sizes of recorders have a gentle, hollow sound.   (p. 332)

REQUINTO *See* JAROCHO ENSEMBLE.

SNARE DRUM   A small cylinder-shaped drum. The snare drum has a flat surface on top made of calfskin or plastic. Several thin metal coils, or snares, are stretched across the bottom. The player strikes the drum with wooden sticks.

Many different sounds may be made on a snare drum. It can play a steady beat or produce a raspy, rolling sound. (p. 132)

STRING BASS   A very large wooden string instrument. It may be plucked with the fingers or played with a bow. The string bass is so tall that the player must stand behind it or sit on a high stool and reach around the front to play it.

The deep, rich voice of the string bass is the lowest of all string instruments.   (p. 122)

TROMBONE   A large brass instrument with one of the loudest voices in the orchestra. The trombone is a long, narrow, curved tube with a bell at one end and a cup-shaped mouthpiece at the other. It has a movable metal tube, called a slide, that lengthens or shortens the tubing.

The trombone can project a huge, brilliant sound, but its soft voice is mellow. It can play the notes fifth graders can sing but can also go much lower.   (p. 122)

TRUMPET   The smallest brass instrument. It has a bell at one end and a cup-shaped mouthpiece at the other. There are three valves, or buttons, on top.

In its loudest voice, the trumpet has an important-sounding, brilliant tone. It can also sound soft, warm, and sweet. Most of the trumpet notes can be sung by fifth graders.   (p. 122)

TUBA The largest brass instrument, with a very large bell that usually points upward. The tuba is so heavy that it may be set on a metal stand while the player sits behind it to blow into the cup-shaped mouthpiece.

The tuba's low notes, the lowest of any brass instrument, are deep and dark sounding. The higher ones are hearty and warm. (p. 122)

VIOLA A wooden string instrument. It looks like a large violin and is played in the same way.

The viola sounds a lot like a violin, but it can play lower notes and has a deeper, darker tone. (p. 122)

VIOLIN A small wooden string instrument that is held under the chin. The player plays it with a bow or plucks it with the fingers.

The violin has many different voices, from a beautiful "singing" quality to a bright, playful, chirping sound. It can play the notes fifth graders sing but can go much higher as well. (p. 122)

ZAMPOÑA (sahm POH nyah) An Andean panpipe that is played by blowing across and into the rims of the tubes, like blowing into soda bottles.

Since the notes on a panpipe are limited, the player can play only those melodic notes that lie in the range of the instrument. (p. 176)

GLOSSARY

AB form (p. 34) A musical plan that has two different parts, or sections.

ABA form (p. 36) A musical plan that has three sections. The first and last sections are the same. The middle section is different.

accidental (p. 85) A sign in music notation used to designate a chromatically altered note. The most common accidentals are sharps, flats, and naturals.

accompaniment (p. 62) Music that supports the sound of the featured performer(s).

ballad (p. 214) A popular song that tells a story.

beat (p. 67) A repeating pulse that can be felt in some music.

brass (p. 122) A group of wind instruments, including trumpets, French horns, trombones, and tubas.

cadence (p. 29) A group of chords or notes at the end of a phrase or piece.

chamber music (p. 123) Music written for small groups, often having only one voice or instrument for each part, as in a string quartet.

chord (p. 114) Three or more different tones played or sung together.

chromatic scale (p. 85) A consecutive succession of twelve half tones.

coda (p. 65) A "tail" or short section added at the end of a piece of music.

composer (p. 19) A person who creates music by putting sounds together in his or her own way.

concerto (p. 124) A composition written for solo instrument(s) with orchestra.

contour (p. 26) The "shape" of a melody, made by the way it moves upward and downward in steps and leaps, and by repeated tones.

countermelody (p. 52) A melody that is played or sung at the same time as the main melody.

descant (p. 54) A countermelody that decorates the main tune, often soaring above the melody of the song.

duet (p. 100) A composition written for two performers.

dynamics (p. 127) The loudness and softness of sound (*f, mf, mp,* <, >, and so on).

ensemble (p. 123) A group of players or singers.

form (p. 36) The overall structure, or plan, of a piece of music.

gamelan (p. 134) Ensembles consisting of gongs, gong-chimes, metallophones, and drums, found in Indonesia, Malaysia, and in scattered places around the Western world.

glissando (p. 65) A continuous movement from one pitch to another.

half step (p. 85) On a keyboard, the distance between one key and the next, black or white.

harmony (p. 58) Two or more different tones sounding at the same time.

improvise (p. 117) Making up music as it is being performed.

interval (p. 111) The distance from one tone to another.

introduction (p. 64) Music played before the main part of a composition begins.

leap (p. 20) To move from one tone to another, skipping over the tones in between.

major scale (p. 85) An arrangement of eight tones, from lower to higher, according to the following pattern of steps or intervals: whole, whole, half, whole, whole, whole, half.

measure (p. 14) A grouping of beats set off by bar lines.

melodic rhythm (p. 40) The rhythm of the words.

melody (p. 20) A line of single tones that moves upward, downward, or repeats.

meter (p. 7) The way beats of music are grouped, often in sets of two or in sets of three.

meter signature (p. 81) The numerical symbol, such as $\frac{2}{4}$ or $\frac{3}{4}$, that tells how many beats are in a measure (top number) and the kind of note that gets one beat (bottom number).

minor scale (p. 84) Several arrangements of eight tones following a pattern of whole and half steps. For example, the natural minor: whole, half, whole, whole, half, whole, whole.

mood (p. 32) The feeling that a piece of music gives. The *mood* of a lullaby is quiet and gentle.

movement (p. 124) Each of the smaller, self-contained sections (usually three or four) that together make up a symphony, concerto, string quartet, and so on.

opera (p. 32)   A theatrical production combining drama, vocal and orchestral music, costumes, scenery, and sometimes dance.

oratorio (p. 172)   A musical drama for voices and orchestra, often based on a religious narrative; usually performed without scenery or action.

ostinato (p. 41)   A rhythm or melody pattern that repeats throughout a piece or a section of a piece.

overture (p. 170)   An instrumental introduction to an opera, oratorio, or other work; the term is sometimes given to an independent orchestral composition.

partner songs (p. 58)   Two or more different songs that can be sung at the same time to create harmony.

pentatonic (p. 82)   Music based on a five-tone scale. A common pentatonic scale corresponds to tones 1, 2, 3, 5, and 6 of the major scale.

percussion (p. 130)   A group of pitched or indefinite pitched instruments that are played by striking with mallets, beaters, and so on, or by shaking.

phrase (p. 26)   A melodic idea that acts as a complete thought, something like a sentence.

pizzicato (p. 64)   On a string instrument, the plucking of the strings.

quartet (p. 99)   A composition for four voices or instruments, each having a separate part; a group of four singers or instrumentalists, each playing or singing a different part.

range (p. 94)   In a melody, the span from the lowest tone to the highest tone.

refrain (p. 90)   The part of a song that repeats, using the same melody and words.

register (p. 94)   The pitch (highness or lowness of a tone) location of a group of tones. If the group of tones are all high sounds, they are in a high *register*. If the group of tones are all low sounds, they are in a low *register*.

repeated tones (p. 20)   Two or more tones in a row that have the same sound.

retrograde (p. 61)   A melody, or motive, read backwards.

rhythm pattern (p. 81)   A combination of sounds and silences in the same or differing lengths.

rondo (p. 43)   A form in which the A section alternates with two contrasting sections, creating a plan of ABACA.

root (p. 114)   The tone on which a chord is built.

round (p. 60)   A follow-the-leader process in which all sing the same melody but start at different times.

scale (p. 84)   An arrangement of pitches from lower to higher according to a specific pattern of intervals or steps.

score (p. 126)   The musical notation of a composition, with each of the instrumental (or vocal) parts shown in vertical alignment.

shanty (p. 216)   A sailor's work song.

steady beat (p. 40)   Regular pulses.

step (p. 20)   To move from one tone to another without skipping tones in between.

strings (p. 122)   A term used to refer to stringed instruments that are played by bowing, plucking, or strumming.

strong beat (p. 68)   The first beat in a measure.

symphony orchestra (p. 18)   In Western art music, an ensemble consisting of multiple strings plus an assortment of woodwinds, brass, and percussion instruments.

tempo (p. 69)   The speed of the beat in music.

texture (p. 52)   The way melody and harmony go together: a melody alone, two or more melodies together, or a melody with chords.

theme (p. 33)   An important melody that occurs several times in a piece of music.

tone color (p. 98)   The special sound that makes one instrument or voice sound different from another.

trio (p. 101)   A composition for three voices or instruments, each having a separate part; a group of three singers or instrumentalists, each playing or singing a different part.

unison (p. 112)   The same pitch.

variation (p. 48)   Music that changes a theme in some important ways.

vocables (p. 95)   Syllables that do not have particular meaning.

whole step (p. 85)   On a keyboard, the distance between any two keys with a single key between.

woodwinds (p. 122)   A term used to refer to wind instruments, now or originally made of wood.

CLASSIFIED INDEX

SONG INDEX

Photograph and Illustration Credits

Acknowledgments

Credit and appreciation are due publishers and copyright owners for use of the following:

"A Camel Dances" from FABLES © 1980 by Arnold Lobel. Harper & Row.

Four on the Floor (snippets) by Libby Larsen.

"Long Trip" from SELECTED POEMS by Langston Hughes. Copyright 1926 by Alfred A. Knopf Inc. and renewed 1954 by Langston Hughes. Reprinted by permission of the publisher.

"After a Freezing Rain" from OUT IN THE DARK AND THE DAYLIGHT by Aileen Fisher. c 1980 Aileen Fisher. Used by permission of HarperCollins Publishers.

"In a Retreat Among Bamboos" from THE JADE MOUNTAIN: A CHINESE ANTHOLOGY, translated by Witter Bynner from the texts of Kiang Kang-Hu. Copyright 1926 and renewed 1954 by Alfred A. Knopf, Inc.

"Washington" by Nancy Byrd Turner from CHILD LIFE MAGAZINE. Copyright 1930, 1958 by Rand McNally & Co. Used with permission.

"A Song of Always" from NOW WE BEGIN by Marian J. and Efraim M. Rosenzweig.

The editors of Silver Burdett Ginn have made every attempt to verify the sources of "Tumba," "Everybody Loves Saturday Night," and "Wagoner's Lad," but were unable to do so. We believe them to be in the public domain.

Every effort has been made to locate all copyright holders of material used in this book. If any errors or omissions have occurred, corrections will be made.

Photograph and Illustration Credits

All photographs are by Silver Burdett Ginn (SBG) unless otherwise noted.

Cover: Jean Tuttle. 2: Maria Stroster. 4–6: Caleb Brown. 7–9: Lori Lohstoeter. 10–11: Charles Campbell/West Light; *art* Bernard Adnet. 12–13: Courtesy Navajo Gallery; *art* Bernard Adnet. 14–15: Chip Henderson Muir; *art* Sergio Baradat. 16–17: Robert Kelley/Life Magazine © Time Warner, Inc.; *art* Lisa Adams. 18: Joseph Viesti/VIESTI ASSOCIATES. 19: The Granger Collection; *border* The Design Library, New York. 18–19: Steven Salerno. 20–21: Sara Anderson. 23–24: Robert Levy. 24–25: *border* The Design Library, New York; *art* Yvonne Buchanan. 25: *m.t.* Smith Garner/The Stock Market; *m.b.* Jose L. Pelaez/The Stock Market. 26–27: Greg Voth. 28–29: Peter Hannan. 30–31: Harry Pederson/SuperStock; *art* Stephen Moscowitz. 32: The Granger Collection. 33: Culver Pictures. 32–33: *art* Sergio Baradat. 34–35: Michelle Barnes. 36–37: Mercedes McDonald. 38: Steve Vidler/Leo deWys, Inc.; *inset* H. Ashford Collection/Michael Ochs Archive. 38–39: Bernard Adnet, Cindy Lindgren. 39: SuperStock. 40: Gwendolyn Wong, Bernard Adnet. 41: *Photograph* courtesy "See Me, Share My World," a global education program of CHILDREACH PLAN INTERNATIONAL; *art* Bernard Adnet. 44–45: Jennifer W. Lester; Richard High. 46–47: *bkgd.* The Design Library, New York; Carolyn George/National Dance Institute; *art* Richard High. 48–49: Juliette Borda. 50–51: *bkgd.* Tim Bieber/The Image Bank. *l. & m.* The Granger Collection. 52–53: Bernard Borda. 54: *l.* Robert Landau/West Light; *m.* Bob Waterman/West Light; *r.* Craig Aurness/West Light. 55: *t.* Bill Ross/West Light; *b.l.* Bob Waterman/West Light; *r.* Robert Landau/West Light. 56–57: Michael McLaughlin. 58–59: Patti McConville/The Image Bank; *art* Bernard Adnet. 60–61: Bernard Adnet. 62–63: Jack E. Davis. 64–65: *Photograph* courtesy Libby Larsen; *art* Rene Zamic. 66–67: *bkgd.* D. Lawrence/Panoramic Stock Images; *art* Bernard Adnet. 67: UPI/The Bettmann Archive. 68–69: Janice Edelman-Lee. 70–71: Bernard Adnet. 71: The Fog Warning, 1885. Winslow Homer. U.S. 1836–1910. Oil on canvas, 30" x 48". Otis Norcross Fund. Courtesy of Museum of Fine Arts, Boston. 94.72. 72–73: James Swanson. 74–75: *bkgd.* SuperStock. 75: *l.* Steve Vidler/Leo deWys, Inc.; *r.* Paul Fusco/Magnum. 76–77: Bernard Adnet. 77: Paula Laraia/LGI Photos. 78–79: Tracy Zungola. 79: Plantation Scene. Unknown. American, 19th century. Watercolor on paper, circa 1800–1820. 80–81: Michael Ochs Archive. 82–83: Private Collection/Scala/Art Resource, New York; *art* Bernard Adnet. 84–85: Campbell Laird. 86–87: Ket Tom. 88–89: Juliette Borda. 90–91: Sara Schwartz. 92–93: SuperStock; *art* Grace De Vito. 94: Bill Barnes for SBG. 94–95: *bkg.* W. Cody/West Light; *art* Bernard Adnet. 96: Art Resource, New York. 97: Culver Pictures. 98–99: Joe Vanderbos. 101: Michael Ochs Archive; *art* Bernard Adnet. 102: Stephen Marks/The Image Bank. 104–105: Bernard Adnet. 106: *t.l.* Charles Gupton/The Stock Market; *b.l.* Rico Rozario/Redferns/Retna Ltd.; *b.r.* Sylvain Grandadam/Tony Stone Images, New York. 106–107 Melanie Marder-Parks. 108–109: Wayne Vincent. 110–111: Jennie Oppenheimer. 112–113: Tony Freeman/PhotoEdit; Stephen Moscowitz. 114–115: Richard Downs. 116: Hilaire Cavanaugh/Tony Stone Images, New York. 117: *l.* Michael Salas/The Image Bank; *r.* Peterson/Liaison International. 116–117: Diane Borowski. 118–119: SuperStock. 120: Steve Skjold for SBG. l21: *t.* Historical Pictures Collection, Stock Montage, Inc.; *b.* Culver Pictures. 120–121: *bkgd.* W. Cody/West Light. 122: Peggy Tagel. 125: Historical Pictures Collection, Stock Montage, Inc; *art* Bernard Adnet. 126–127: Albert Lemant. 128: Bernard Adnet. 130: Cameramann International. 131: Richard Pasley/Stock, Boston; *art* Brian Dugan. 132: J. Ramey/The Image Bank; *art* Brian Dugan. 133: Frilet/Sipa Press; *art* Brian Dugan. 134: © 1995 Chuck O'Rear/Woodfin Camp & Associates; *art* Brian Dugan. 135: John Launois/Black Star; *art* Brian Dugan. 136: Roger Huyssen. 138: *l.* James Simon/Tony Stone Images, New York; *r.* Robert E. Daemmrich/Tony Stone Images, New York; *art* Juliette Borda. 139: *l.* Robert Daemmrich; *r.* Myrleen Ferguson/PhotoEdit; *art* Juliette Borda. 140–141: *bkgd.* Duclos Guichard/Gouver/Gamma Liaison; *inset* David Madison/Duomo; *art* Lisa Blackshear. 142–145: Lin Wilson. 145: Map, 1961. Jasper Johns. Oil on canvas, 6' 6" x 10' 3/8" (198.2 cm x 314.7 cm). The Museum of Modern Art, New York. Gift of Mr. and Mrs. Robert C. Scull. Photograph © 1993. The Museum of Modern Art, New York. 146–147: Jim Dryden. 148–149: Eugene Kagansky. 150–151: Karen Blessen. 152–155: RAGS Photography; *art* David McLimans. 156–157: Peter Cunningham, courtesy Mendola, Ltd; *art* Dan Yaccarino. 158–159: Copyright © by Universal City Studios, Inc. Courtesy of MCA Publishing Rights, a division of MCA, Inc. Photograph: Kobal Collection; *art* Brian Dugan. 164–165: Bernard Adnet. 167: Martha Swope; *art* Brian Cairns. 168: Robert Marshak; *art* Gil Adams. 171: Winnie Klotz; *art* Diane Teske Harris. 175: *t.* Courtesy of Agency for Performing Arts; *m.* Dave Allocca/Retna, Ltd.; *b.* Veryl Oakland/Retna, Ltd.; *art* Peggy Tagel. 176–177: Melanie Marder-Parks. 178–179: Charlie Shaw. 180–181: Mike Reed. 182–183: *bkgd.* Murray & Associates/Tony Stones Images, New York; *inset* Jack Vartoogian; *art* Troy Thomas. 184–185: Jack Vartoogian; *art* David Coulson. 186: *l.* John Elk/Bruce Coleman; *r.* John Running/Black Star; *art* Melissa Joachim. 187: *l.* © Ray Hunold/Photo Researchers, Inc; *r.* Jean Gavmy/Magnum; *art* Melissa Joachim. 188: Bernard Adnet. 189: The Poet Lin Bu Wandering in the Moonlight. Hanging scroll. Ink & slight color on paper, h. 156.5. Du Jin, Chinese, active ca. 1465–1505, Ming Dynasty. © The Cleveland Museum of Art, John L. Severance Fund, 54.582. 190–191: David Coulson, Jean & Mou-sien Tseng. 192: Theo Westenberger/Liaison International, photograph courtesy of American Indian Dance Theater; *art* Raphaelle Goethals. 194–195: Bernard Adnet. 196–197: Philadelphia Historical Society/SuperStock; *art* John P. Genzo. 198: Michael Ochs Archive; *art* Patricia DeWitt-Grush & Robin DeWitt. 199: Library of Congress. 200: Robert McElroy/Gamma Liaison. 201: Janice Edelman-Lee; Sara Schwartz. 202–203: Jurgen Vogt/The Image Bank; Patricia DeWitt-Grush & Robin DeWitt. 204–205: Lindy Burnett. 206: AP/Wide World Photos, Inc.; *art* Paul Janovsky. 208–209: Dan Picasso. 210–211: Beth Gwinn/Retna, Ltd. 212–213: Michael McGurl. 214: His Hammer in His Hand. Palmer C. Haydn. From the collection of The Museum of African American Art, Palmer C. Hayden Collection. Gift of Mirian A. Hayden. Photograph by Armando Solis; *art* Burton Morris. 216–217: Diane Teske Harris. 218–219: Stephen Schudlich. 220–221: Lawrence Migdale/Tony Stone Images, New York; *art* Gwendolyn Wong. 223: *bkgd.* John Ramey/The Image Bank; *inset* By Dawn's Early Light. E. Percy Moran. The Peale Museum, Baltimore City Life Museums; *art* Ryle Smith. 226–227: Jeff Hunter/The Image Bank; *art* April Blair Stewart. 228: The Granger Collection; *art* Wayne Vincent. 229: Ruby Green Singing, 1928. James Chapin. Oil on canvas. Norton Gallery of Art. 230: UPI/The Bettmann Archive; *art* Bernard Adnet. 232: *bkgd.* Robert Brenner/PhotoEdit. l. Stockman/International Stock Photos; *r.* Miwako/International Stock Photos; *art* Robert Roper. 233: l. Philip Little/International Stock Photos; *r.* Ronn Maratea/International Stock Photos. 234–235: Bernard Adnet, Paulette Bogan. 236–237: Bernard Adnet. 238–239: Jack E. Davis. 240–243: Mary Thelen. 244: *art* Bernard Adnet. 246: Courtesy of Texas Boys Choir; *art* David Coulson. 247: David Young Wolff/PhotoEdit; *art* David Coulson. 248–250 *art* Bernard Adnet. 251: *bkgd.* The Granger Collection; *art* Bernard Adnet. 252–253: Suzanne L. Murphy/DDB Stock; *art* Bernard Adnet. 254–255: Odette Lupis; *art* Bernard Adnet. 257: *t.l. & t.r.* Cameramann International; *b.* Dave Bartruff; *art* Bernard Adnet. 258–259: Bernard Adnet. 260–267: Joann Adinolfi. 268: Farida Zaman. 270–271: Lauren Scheuer. 272–273: Michael McGurl. 274–275: Michael McLaughlin. 276–277: Dan Uaccarino. 278–279: Mark McConnel. 280: Sarah Stone/Tony Stone Images, New York; *art* Jonathan Milne. 281: *bkgd.* H. Wendler/The Image Bank; *art* Jonathan Milne. 282–283: Bernard Adnet. 284–285: Kiley Jenkins, Monica Stevenson. 287: Mother and Child. Mary Cassatt. The Roland P. Murdock Collection. Wichita Art Museum, Wichita, Kansas. Photograph, Henry Nelson. 288: *bkgd.* Dave Reede/First Light; *inset* Hot Shots; *art* Raphaelle Goethals. 289: *bkgd.* Stock Imagery; *inset* Steve Vidler/Leo deWys, Inc. 290–291: *inset* Cameramann International; *art* Cindy Lindgren. 292–293: Joseph Nettis/Stock, Boston; *art* Mary Lempa. 294: Willi Dolder/Tony Stone Images, New York; *art* Robert Roper. 296–297: *bkgd.* Pete Saloutos/The Stock Market; *inset* Benn Mitchell/The Stock Market; *art* Bernard Adnet. 298–299: Craig Smallish. 300–301: Peggy Tagel. 302–303: *bkgd.* Tom Parker/Tony Stone Images, New York. 302: *inset* Philip & Karen Smith/Tony Stone Images, New York. 303: Mark Harmel/FPG International. 304–305: Steve Schudlich. 306–307: Yvonne Buchanan. 308–309: Cindy Lindgren. 310: National Museum of American Art, Washington DC/Art Resource, New York; *art* Bernard Adnet. 311: Jean & Mou-sien Tseng. 312: Color Box/FPG International; *art* Nelle Davis, Ted Cooper. 313: *l., m.* Brian Seed/Tony Stone Images, New York; *r.* Dmitri Kessel/The Stock Market. *art* Tod Cooper. 314: The Bridgeman Art Library; *art* Michael Radencich. 315: Rivelli/The Image Bank. 316–317: *art* Linda Frichtel. 318: E. Nagele/FPG International; *art* Susan Greenstein. 319: Robert L. Goddard/Picture Perfect. 320–321: Jennie Oppenheimer. 322–323: Charles Peale. 24–325: *bkgd.* The Granger Collection; *inset* Special Collections in Music, The University of Maryland, College Park; *art* Bernard Adnet. 327: Paramount Pictures; *art* Gwendolyn Wong. 330–331: Terry Kovalaki. 330–331: Terry Kovalaki.

Sound Bank Photographs 334: *Charango*- Robert Houser for SBG. 336: *Jarocho Ensemble*- Bill Albrecht for SBG; Ann Summa for SBG; *Jarana*- Courtesy of Zazhil/Bill Albrecht for SBG. 337: *Native American Flute*- The Shrine to Music Museum/University of South Dakota. 339: *Zampona*- Robert Houser for SBG.

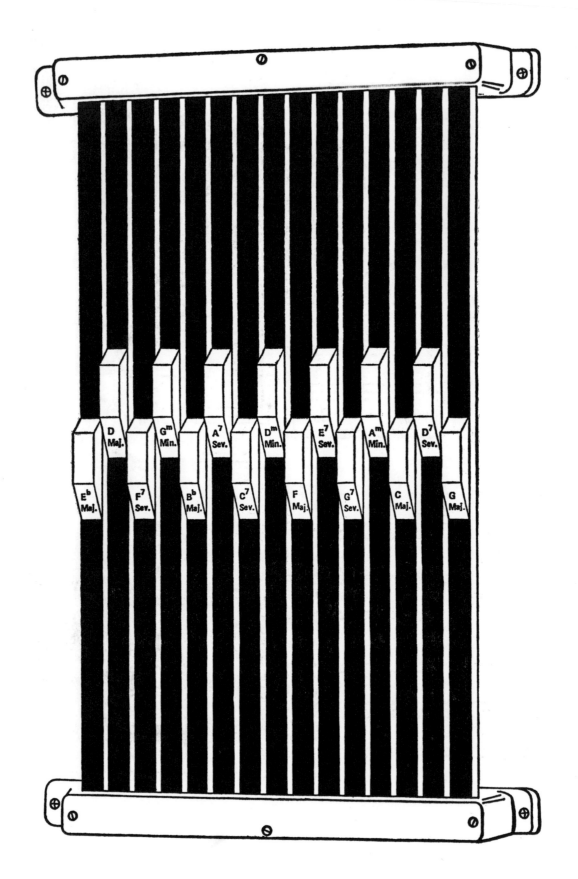